Happy Dog / Happy Owner Book

How to Recognize and Handle the Emotional Problems of Your Dog

by MORDECAI SIEGAL

1984 — First Edition — First Printing

HOWELL BOOK HOUSE Inc.
230 Park Avenue
New York, N.Y. 10169

For my son T.J.

How do you say thank you for the sunshine?

Part of the text of this book was published
under the title of *Mordecai Siegal's Happy Pet/Happy Owner Book*
copyright © 1978 by Mordecai Siegal.

Permission to quote material from:
CANINE DIETETICS, copyright © 1975 by
Mark Morris Associates, Topeka, Kansas.

Gaine's BASIC GUIDE TO CANINE NUTRITION
(Fourth Edition) by Robert W. Mellentin,
copyright © 1977 by
General Foods Corporation, White Plains, New York.

Library of Congress Cataloging in Publication Data

Siegal, Mordecai.
Happy dog/happy owner book.

Bibliography: p. 143
1. Dogs. 2. Dogs—Behavior. I. Title.
SF427.S59 1984   636.7'70887   84-6667
ISBN 0-87605-556-0

Contents

Acknowledgments

For the excruciating silence and for the use of her imagination, I wish to express deepest gratitude to my wife Vicki, whose insistence and assistance brought this book about.

Thank you Bart Campbell of ALPO and also to Don Hyman for your help and cooperation.

Thank you, Mark Morris, Jr., for the use of your research, charts and other materials.

To Steve Willett, Director of Gaines Professional Services, and to Tom O'Shea of Gaines Dog Care Center, for allowing me to use their charts, nutritional material and wonderful, wonderful photographs.

With admiration and gratitude to Captain Arthur Haggerty, director of the Captain Haggerty School for Dogs.

To Carol Lea Benjamin, author and all round good person, thank you and Oliver for the photos.

A special note of gratitude to Nancy Strauss, Director of People Training for Dogs in New York.

Introduction

I HOWLED all night long for the first week of my life. My parents let me cry it out for fear of "spoiling" me. This probably accounts for my empathy with puppies and the fact that I stay up late every night. It's not difficult to look at the world through puppy-colored glasses. Sometimes I feel like I'm wagging an invisible tail. In other words, I identify quite strongly with dogs more, perhaps, than I should.

To write about dogs is to write about all the important things in life. To wit: love, fear, anxiety, joy, pleasure, friendship, death, birth, God and existence itself. Tolstoy and I write about the same things . . . it's just a question of style.

Everything that a human being experiences in a lifetime can be expressed through the eternal relationship between humans and their pets. It's as important a subject as any and I've learned that it's most important to a great many people. This is a book about the emotional life of your dog. It only deals with human emotions to the extent that they are created by the behavior of dogs. Yes, I believe that dogs experience emotions and much of their behavior stems from these emotions. I also believe that their emotions are often created by human behavior.

Please do not misunderstand. It is not my intention to apply what is known about "human" psychology to the behavior and experience of animals. That does not work as a method of understanding dog behavior and I reject it completely. Dog behavior is a species' specific set of responses and actions that are unique to the family *Canidae* (with some variation) which consists of dogs, wolves, jackals, foxes, maned wolf, raccoon dog, and bat-eared fox.

According to R. F. Ewer in her book *The Carnivores*: "The Canidae are medium-sized carnivores, adapted to swift running on relatively open terrain. They live mainly, but by no means exclusively, on flesh and possess crushing molar teeth suitable for dealing with vegetable food. The canine teeth are fairly large but not highly specialised: they are not particularly sharp and not much flattened and are a good all-purposes weapon, not specifically adapted to delivering a highly oriented death bite. The Canidae are cosmopolitan in distribution . . ."

To that I would add that dogs are possessed of a highly refined set of behaviors having evolved over the millennia into a unique catalog of inherited actions and responses which are predictable. What is not predictable is the impact of environmental influence. A dog that defends its home aggressively will not attack a stranger when he or she is introduced properly by its master. That is predictable dog behavior. But if that same animal were abused in any serious manner or traumatized by an event, its behavior with a stranger is unpredictable no matter what the master says or does.

I believe that dogs experience intense emotions when confronted with circumstances not meant for their expectations in the natural state. For instance, inadequate exercise can stress a dog to a high degree and create destructive chewing or biting behavior. Constant loneliness and isolation can actually drive a dog mad. Exposure to these circumstances are, in various degrees, violations of their genetically programmed needs. Rather than refer to the resulting behavior as neurotic (a medical term used by and for humans) I would say emotions are formed that could lead to abnormal behavior and perhaps a permanent personality change. Would Mozart have composed *The Magic Flute* had he taken a subway during the rush hour? Can a dog remain true to his sweet and magical nature if forced to endure *undoggable* realities? Caught between canine behavior and the human world dogs can become quite emotional and need understanding and some help from a friend.

The emotional entanglements of dogs and people may seem very funny unless you happen to be one of the parties to the entanglement. Depressed dogs, obese dogs, phobic dogs are only the tip of the emotional icebergs that can pervade an otherwise happy household. When dogs become destructive or refuse to be housebroken it's time

7

to come to grips with their emotional problems. It's time to find out who your pet really is.

For too long the dog owner has had to stumble around blindly in hopes that things will right themselves or else just learn to live with the unlivable. Unfortunately, fools and their dogs are soon parted; and feelings, emotional connections, and even lives are squandered in the wake.

The answers to your dog's problems are as different and unique as one dog from another. There are no set answers to any behavior difficulties in human or animal life. What works for one will not necessarily work for another. The human family might as well throw away preconceived notions, old formulations, amateur advice, and his or her own instinctive behavior. Where, you ask, does that leave us?

Assuming the relationship with your dog is important, the solution for an emotional problem requires human effort and understanding. We must be able to evaluate a dog's behavior as abnormal or normal—abnormal for a dog! All too often a dog will seem to be behaving strangely. However, its behavior, which is genetically organized by nature, may be absolutely correct for that species despite the fact that it conflicts with human values. *What is required of the dog owner is a working knowledge of dog behavior so that elements in the environment which stimulate unpleasant behavior can be modified, eliminated, or at the very least, understood.* If an animal's behavior is evaluated as abnormal when compared to its true nature, there is little the layman can do outside of seeking professional help. Some problems can be solved by professional dog trainers and handlers; others require the services of clinicians working with behavior modification. Fortunately, most emotional problems suffered by pet dogs can be solved by understanding what's normal for a dog and why. With that information, we can set out to alter the living conditions that create the problem.

Each chapter of this book reflects an important category that is of vital concern to all dog owners. The subject is discussed in the context of the emotional problems of the animal. This is immediately followed by a story situation that best illustrates the plight of the animal and its effect on the human involved. Each vignette is a composite of case studies representing many combined people, dogs and situations. It is hoped that these stories will entertain as well as illuminate.

Before obedience training, before the leash and collar, before the retrieved stick and rubber ball with the bell inside, there was inherited behavior, genetically organized for life in the wild state. The evolution of dogs never took into account the plus and minus of human intervention. Learning to recognize and cope with inherited canine behavior can make the difference between a happy or emotionally charged dog. And a happy dog creates a happy owner.

The puppy experience is like no other. To miss it
is to miss the rainbow side of dogs.   *M. Siegal*

1

Hushpuppy Nights

Puppyhood

Once a puppy whispers in your ear, life is never the same. Baby dogs are like love machines whose mainsprings take a full year to unwind to a steady, rhythmic pace. A little wet nose, a slurping tongue, four paws, and a metronome tail click madly away in an indefatigable ode to joy. The puppy experience is like no other. To miss it is to miss the rainbow side of doghood. Although their tiny teeth bite like sharp needles and their piddling on the carpet is nerve-wracking as is the all-night howl of a homesick youngster, puppy pleasures more than compensate. The busybody waddle of a wide-eyed puppy and its cuddling desire to crawl through your armpit into your ear and lick out the last ounce of love is not only irresible, it is addictive.

To understand your puppy is to understand the dog that he will be. There are those occasions when a puppy can get the most loving human into a state of frustration which can easily turn into rage. Understanding the little dog's true nature helps avoid destructive anger while you are finding solutions and answers.

As in human infancy, the early phase of a dog's life involves physical growth and mental development. Human childhood is a long stage, perhaps the longest in nature, and under the best circumstances involves two adult parents protecting, providing for, and instructing the child. Infancy to adulthood is compacted into one year in the life of a dog.

In the first three weeks of puppyhood, the young dog develops all of his sensory abilities plus many of his motor capacities. From the beginning of the fourth week until the end of the seventh week, the puppy enters a period of socialization the consequences of which affect his behavior for the rest of his life. During this critical period of socialization, the dog's environment plays a major role in how the animal will be able to adapt to human beings (and their demands) and the presence of other dogs. During this four-week period, the brain and the central nervous system are developing into full maturity. Interaction with littermates and the mother teach the puppy indelible lessons about "pack existence." This canine socialization helps them create attachments to other puppies and produces an animal that will adjust easily with other dogs as an adult. If, in addition, the puppy is handled by a human being at least twice a day between four and seven weeks of age, the dog will also adapt readily to humans with ease and comfort. Thus, by the end of the seventh week, the animal will become adaptive to dogs and humans and will get along well with both. It is then time to remove the puppy from the litter before the question of dominance and subordination is settled within the litter itself.

Beginning in the eighth week, some pups begin to bully others, while some become timid, shy and even terror-ridden. The issue of who is dominant and who is subordinate is settled by puppy fights, the competition for food, and best placement for the mother's body warmth. The largest male often becomes the dominant animal at the expense of the other dogs who in turn work out their dominant or subordinate relationships with each other. These placements in the pack structure become permanent in the minds of the dogs. If the litter remains together for up to sixteen weeks, the order of dominance and subordination becomes absolute. Often a dominant dog will become an overly aggressive animal, untrainable or unsuitable for a pet/human relationship. An undersized puppy may be last in the pack structure and develop into an extremely timid or shy animal which has negative consequences when he becomes an adult dog living as a pet.

Between eight and sixteen weeks personality based on dominance and subordination takes shape. In a pack environment, the young dog takes his place in the social structure until circumstances dictate the necessity for change. Anytime after six months, a dog is physically capable of mating and renewing the cycle. When a human family takes a puppy into their home, this cycle is still ongoing, with the human environment substituting for the canine factors. Ideally, a pet dog should take a subordinate position in relation to his human family (or pack). This can come about only if the dog is adaptive to humans and if the humans in the family take the leadership position (without becoming overbearing). When the pet owner understands this he or she is prepared for what comes naturally. In the beginning, all puppy behavior is based on instinct and the predilection toward pack structure.

Marjorie and William Sweden drove 400 miles through the heart of New England to acquire what they hoped would be the most perfect Irish Wolfhound east of the Mississippi. They had to answer many tough and demanding questions in order to pass the muster of the cantankerous breeder, a weather-beaten Mrs. Elvira Hagerstrom. "Will the dog be left alone much of the time?" "Do you have a veterinarian?" Can you afford the dog's appetite? He eats a great deal, you know." "Will you attempt to campaign him and get him his AKC Championship?" "Do you promise *not* to mate him with a bitch not of his own breed?"

On their honor to do their best for God and the entire race of Irish Wolfhounds, the Swedens felt as though they had just won a child-custody fight. Mrs. Hagerstrom of Baskerville Kennels reluctantly turned the curly-coated puppy over to the care of the excited couple, but not without a skeptical once-over that would have turned any first sergeant green with envy. The Swedens were now the proud owners of Baskerville's Juggernaut of Galway's Glen-in-the-Moss. They decided to call him Jughead—privately, that is, and about five miles away from Elvira Hagerstrom's icy stare. The large, sweet puppy responded happily to the call name. But the Swedens kept looking over their shoulders every time they said the name "Jughead." They expected Mrs. Hagerstrom to come flying at them on a broom like the Wicked Witch of the North. Little did they know that the flinty old breeder liked them and knew they would make excellent Irish Wolfhound people. However, they had quite a lot to learn. There was much ahead of them.

The yowling and the whining seemed to vibrate all the steel girders of 73rd Street, east of Park Avenue. It was two in the morning, and the puppy hadn't stopped crying since the lights went out at midnight. Bill and Marj stared at the ceiling from their bed confident that they could tough it out. They read in a book that they weren't supposed to give in to the dog's whimpers, cries, yipes, barks, growls, or rar-rars. Jughead was an intense rar-rarer. He brought rar-raring to an art form. The puppy's high-pitched rar-rars moved upstairs from the kitchen, where he was confined, to the bedroom, where the unhappy dog owners suffered privately in the dark. Marjorie dug her nails into her palms as Bill methodically ground his bicuspids flat.

"That's it," he muttered, rising out of his rosebud sheets like a bear leaving a burning tree. "If this keeps up, we're going to get evicted," he snorted.

Marjorie moaned, "We own the house, Bill."

"I cannot take this any longer. I'm going down there and I'm going to beat that dog within an inch of his life," he shouted as he struggled to find one slipper.

"Maybe a dish of warm milk will do the trick," whispered the exhausted Marjorie.

"What the hell are you whispering about?" demanded Bill. "He's not losing any sleep. The book said we shouldn't indulge the beast. No milk! Just a boot up his rear end."

Clad in his pajamas and armed with one slipper on his left foot, Bill Sweden descended the stairs of his duplex and marched to the barricaded kitchen doorway. He entered the room and frantically felt along the wall for the light switch. His pajama cuff caught on a picture hook and tore the sleeve up to the elbow. As the sleeve was tearing, his unslippered right foot stepped into a pool of liquid with a semisolid object in its center. His foot went sliding as his toes made a heroic effort to dig into the hard, permanently waxed linoleum floor. His trunk hit the floor with a solid thunk, and every part of him slid through the semiliquid mess. The stars came out for an instant, and Bill lay in the dark, staring at the luminescent wall clock telling him it was 2:17.

In a panic, Marjorie ran down the stairs and quickly turned the kitchen light on. Bill was still on the floor, on his back. He looked up at his wife as Juggernaut of Galway's Glen-in-the-Moss licked his nose, his ear, his lips, and his neck. Every inch of his pajamas was drenched in yellow liquid. His hair, right hand, left elbow, and right foot were thickly smeared in unpleasantness.

Marjorie laughed uncontrollably, Jughead wagged his merry tail, and Bill said faintly, "Help."

Puppies do not cry through the first nights in a new home simply because they are willful or self-centered. A domestic dog's instincts are similar to those of his wild cousin, the wolf. If any wild canid should accidentally be separated from the litter or pack as a young pup, its life would be in grave jeopardy. The pup would be vulnerable to natural enemies. It would probably die of hunger since it is too young to hunt and bring down game for food. From the dog's perspective, the first nights in a human situation are fraught with terror. He doesn't know where he is or what's going to happen. Everything familiar is gone. He's been taken away from his littermates, his mother, his kennel, or the short-lived familiarity of a pet-shop environment.

In the few hours spent with his new family, the dog has learned that he is safe in the human presence. When they leave him for the night, his fear of the unknown and his need for mother's warmth gain control and cause him to howl. This is precisely why the puppy yells until he gains human attention. Unfortunately, that attention is often as unpleasant for the little dog as it is for the human. Too much howling usually earns a hollering or a hitting session.

Removed from his familiar territory, his littermates, his mother and even his new pack (the Swedens) poor Jughead felt lost and abandoned in his new home. Although it is not necessary to allow the puppy to sleep in the same bed, it is humane to soothe the dog and try to alleviate his fears. There are several ways to do this. The best method is to use a large cardboard box or crate as a means of bedding the dog in a confined area. Use a high-sided carton so that he cannot crawl out. *Place the box with the dog in it in your bedroom each night so that the puppy is constantly aware of your presence.*

This method is effective for two reasons. First, in the first three or four weeks of the puppy's life, he has no physical ability to eliminate his body wastes. Elimination is accomplished through stimulation by the mother's tongue as she licks her puppies' stomach and genital regions. In those early weeks the puppies learn that no body wastes are allowed to fall into their nest. The mother ingests them, thus maintaining a state of hygiene. By the fourth week, all the puppies leave the nest to eliminate independently. They never relieve themselves inside the nest (if they can help it). This imprinted behavior will be carried over into the puppy's new environment.

Second, within a very short period of time (sometimes within hours), your new puppy accepts you and your family as his new litter (or pack). Therefore, sleeping in the same room is very natural to him and brings into play his imprinted value not to soil his own nest. Jughead adapted to the Swedens almost instantly and regarded them as his family with all of the behavior that accompanies that state of mind. He did not want to be parted from them, but as long as he was, it did not seem unacceptable to relieve himself on their kitchen floor. After all, he was not in his nest, which according to him was either upstairs in their bedroom or back in New England with Elvira Hagerstrom.

Another reason for confining the puppy in a small box is so that he cannot circle around with ease as he does before he defecates. If you decide to allow the puppy's nest to be placed in your bedroom, it is a good idea to close the door just in case he manages to climb out of the carton. A free-roaming puppy will use the entire house for his toilet and may get himself into serious trouble. Because a puppy's stomach and bladder are small, he may have one or two accidents through the night, but at least the mess will be confined to the box, providing he cannot crawl out of it. It may be a good idea to spread newspapers around the bedroom just in case the puppy does get out and relieves himself.

Another way of comforting a puppy so that he will not be too distressed during those awful first nights is to place a ticking alarm clock in the box with him. This simulates his mother's heartbeat and has some good effect. A half-filled hot water bottle wrapped in a towel may make it seem like one of his littermates is with him and also have a soothing effect. A dog's sense of smell is his keenest sense. Therefore, a towel or blanket that has the odor of his last home will be of enormous help in this distressing situation. Dogs remember many things by cataloging odors in their memories. The smell of their last home may be of great comfort. If the puppy is going to be confined in another room, play a radio on low volume or a one-hour recording of your voice on a tape cassette. This, too, may calm the little animal so that all may get a night's sleep.

———————————

At age five months it was hard to think of the growing Jughead as a puppy. He was growing and starting to show some of the largeness associated with Irish Wolfhounds. However, his awkward and gangling manner coupled with that funny way of cocking his head when viewing his first New York bug revealed him as the puppy that he was.

For the first two months, Jughead was never left alone. If Marj or Bill didn't look after him then the maid did. It was a perfect arrangement for a young dog until the night the Swedens were invited to a dinner party on the maid's day off. By now the canine adolescent had endeared himself to his owners with his gentle and affectionate nature. Like all puppies, Jughead was curious about everything and loped around the spacious duplex after anyone that would allow him to follow. Curiosity is the driving force behind all learning. When a puppy waddles away from its litter it is actually a sign of mental and physical growth just as a baby's crawling away from its parents the first time is the first step toward separation and adulthood. Jughead was a curious dog, but the Swedens had no idea just how curious he was. He had completely won their confidence as a good-mannered, well-behaved pet.

The large puppy was prone on the carpet with his face between his two legs, chin flat on the floor, as he watched his family switch off all but two lights. The evening routine was different, and the great puppy knew it immediately. His eyes swiveled in their sockets following the tall humans as they swiftly prepared to leave. The dog knew every detail of movement and action connected to the routine events of the day and night. Whenever the Swedens were going out, the maid was a presence and took charge of the dog's food and other needs. However, this evening the maid was nowhere to be found, and the master and mistress were on their way out. It was different and the

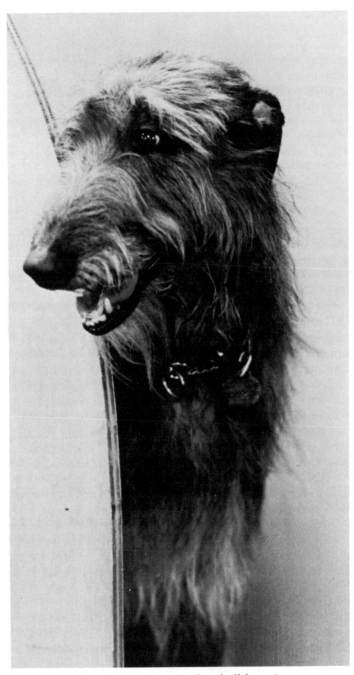

Curiosity is the driving force behind all learning.

M. Siegal

dog knew it instantly. The gangling offspring never moved from his position.

Bill knelt down and squeezed the dog's face lovingly as he told him what a good dog he was and how he should protect the castle from marauders. As the elegant couple went smoothly through the front door, Marj said, "Okay, Juggernaut of Whose's Glen-in-the-Moss, be a good dog and take a long nap." The door closed and the dog was on his own for the first time.

At first there was no sound at all. After two or three minutes, the dog could hear a slight rattle in the heat pipe. He clumsily rose from the carpet and ungracefully bounced slowly to the kitchen to slurp some water and sniff his kibble. Having accomplished that, he plopped down in front of his food bowl and prepared for a nap as he was ordered. The dog almost fell off into a light puppy sleep, but suddenly decided not to do that and sprang to his feet. He checked his food supply to make certain he wouldn't starve. He was in a new state of solitude and there were no guarantees that he would ever see the Swedens again.

Jughead bent down into his bowl and ate two or three kibbles. But they were not satisfying. He felt like having something but didn't really know what. So he decided to eat the bowl. He gripped the large ceramic dish between his teeth and lifted it up from the floor. Of course, all the cereal spilled out onto his nose and then to the floor and partially into his water bowl. Noticing the slight splash that the kibble made, he immediately lost interest in what was in his mouth. He tossed the bowl to the side and jumped when it crashed into several large pieces on the floor. Once he recovered from that surprise, he fixed his attention back on the water bowl. First he sniffed it and then stuck his paw through the water to the bottom. This was very amusing, so he started poking one paw then the other in the water swiftly so that it splashed over much of the floor. The kitchen soon became drenched. The gray-coated pup decided to leave that annoying room because someone had made the floor uncomfortably wet and he was sliding around trying to keep his balance.

It was time for a chew on his white nylon bone, but it was somewhere in a pool of water in the kitchen. Jughead trotted to the front door of the apartment to make sure that his folks weren't standing outside waiting to surprise him at any minute. He sniffed the bottom crack where the door met the saddle. No surprises waiting there for him. It was time to explore and investigate those things that were always forbidden to him as long as some human was around to say no. He trotted to the arch separating the living room from the dining room and sat down like a sphinx gazing into the desert. His tongue hung out the side of his mouth and he panted as he surveyed the spacious room, deciding what to examine first. His panting stopped and he pulled in his tongue as the fringe of the Oriental carpet beckoned with its twisted, ropy fingers. They became a make-believe form of life that could be captured and eaten.

Big puppy swiftly pounced on the carpet's edge and tried to remove the fringe with his rotating paws. This was useless because the stringy material would not submit to his grip. With a high-pitched yowl, he lay on his side and tried to bite the elusive ropes, but they still slid between his teeth and lips. In a cheerful frenzy and with an expression that could be taken for a smirk, Jughead lifted the edge of the carpet with his paws and took a good portion of it in his mouth. This accomplished, he rose to his feet and began to pull for all he was worth. His muscles and bones tensed and set in place as a thousand pounds of biting pressure allowed his newly emerging canine teeth to sink between the expensive fibers of the imported antique carpet. An end table tipped over, one of the two sofas moved, as did a delicate wooden chair, and a porcelain lamp fell and unluckily hit the hardwood surface. The porcelain shattered when the bulb popped. Jughead dropped his grip and ran out of the room. That was the second time someone had tried to frighten him.

In a mad dash he re-entered the living room and attacked the arm of the tweed sofa. The pliant stuffing felt exotically sensual against his tongue and black lips as it twirled out of the shredded tweed and fell to the floor drenched in saliva. Jughead then hauled his bony body up onto the couch and sat comfortably on its soft pillow as he methodically munched the arm down to the inner wood dreaming of ancient wolves and Roman kings. And so the evening went.

Marj Sweden went faint as she managed to get herself to a living-room chair. Bill went to his rifle closet in the den hoping to catch the drug-addict burglar in the midst of his vicious assault on their beautiful home.

"Obviously," he concluded rather hastily, "they were tearing the place up looking for cash or hidden jewelry. I better call the cops. Say, Marj, are you all right?" He went to his wife as tears spilled from her eyes. She pointed to the opposite corner of the room and indicated that someone was behind the large stuffed chair. With rifle in hand, Bill softly approached the forbidding chair as he silently unclicked the safety.

"Oh, my God," he shouted. "It's the dog!" Playfully looking up at Bill and Marj was Jughead. He had momentarily paused from chewing on the corner of the carpet—or rather, what was left of it. It was going to be another long night for dogs and humans.

We tend to classify the entire first year of dogs as puppyhood. This is a very vague and general term which can be misleading. We must be aware of that major portion of the first year known as adolescence. For the pet owner, it is a sometimes marvelous, sometimes wretched period. Although the dog's entire nervous system including brain functions is fully developed by the third week, there is much to accomplish in the coming months. Dogs are genetically programmed with various survival instincts that do not take into account the good "pet life." Adolescence can be loosely defined as that period between the fourth and twelfth months. This is a period of body growth (twenty-four months for the largest breeds), sexual development and the refinement of survival techniques.

The greatest mistake the Sweden family made was to assume that their young dog was capable of being left alone in their home without supervision. Had they known better they would have had someone stay with the animal or simply have confined him to one room such as the kitchen so that he could not damage the rest of the house with his adolescent needs. In the kitchen (or other confinement space), he should have been left with his food, water, toys, and newspapers on the floor for toileting purposes.

Adolescent dogs left alone fluctuate between fear, boredom, and curiosity. Jughead had accepted the Swedens as a substitute for his pack. If the members of the pack leave him alone, even in the comfort of his den (home), it is bound to cause him some degree of anxiety and fear. This will lock into gear some of his survival instincts and be a great factor in his behavior until he is distracted or his emotions are quieted. From Jughead's point of view, how is he to know for sure that his pack is ever going to return—especially if a well-established routine is broken?

The first concern of a dog questioning his survival is his food supply. Jughead checked out his bowl and was satisfied. Although he did become playfully distracted by his water bowl, he felt somewhat secure about food. The next aspect of survival had to do with enemies. The slightest sound could mean an intrusion from a natural enemy or someone intending to violate his territory. This trait explains why a steam pipe noise could be enough to get an adolescent dog in motion. It could very well have been someone knocking at the door or even a telephone ring. All of these factors could have created a state of anxiety or fear which, in turn, sets the dog up for destructive behavior.

Boredom is probably the single most important element of unacceptable behavior in dogs left alone. All dogs become bored when left alone. Only the most well-behaved and those who have been obedience trained can be trusted to leave the house intact. Even then we are talking about a more mature animal. One solution to boredom is getting the dog a companion of his own—another dog or even a cat. Several toys that the dog knows for sure are his can be of great help. A good rawhide or synthetic material bone for chewing is good, as is a thick, tough dog ball manufactured for that purpose. Select a variety of safe, nontoxic (lead-free) toys. A young, curious dog is going to become bored faster and for longer periods of time than a mature dog completely familiar with his environment and territory.

Jughead's fascination with his water bowl was just another manifestation of youthful curiosity, an important part of play. We tend to regard play behavior in humans as well as in animals as a pleasant but frivolous activity with no more than amusement value. Actually, play behavior is a teaching/learning process for the youngster whether he is human, dog, cat, or other mammal.

All of childhood, all of puppyhood and adolescence, is a mental and physical process preparing for independence and self-sufficiency. Even though pet animals have very little to worry about in terms of self-sufficiency, nature still provides the learning process including those involving play. When a litter of puppies or a single young dog plays, it always has something to do with expending energy (exercise), learning how to fight (claiming territory, winning a mate, and confronting natural enemies), prey capture (hunting for food), or escape movements (survival). Puppies rarely hurt one another even though they bite and chew on each other as they roll and tumble in mad exuberance. However, a teething adolescent dog, bored and with a strong desire to play, can virtually destroy the home he lives in without meaning any harm.

First Jughead experienced a mild state of anxiety over the break in his routine. Then he quickly became bored. Next, he was swept up

Boredom is probably the single most important element of unacceptable behavior in dogs left alone.   *Carol Benjamin*

in a desire to satisfy his curiosity by exploring the forbidden areas of his territory and, last, he participated in play behavior that dealt a deadly blow to the Swedens' apartment. The fringe of the carpet became an exercise in prey capture, and the attack upon the furniture was a learning experience concerning attacking an enemy (albeit an imaginary one). Chewing up the couch and armchair can probably be attributed to a teething problem. It was all avoidable. All they had to do was confine the dog to one puppy-proofed room.

At five months of age, a dog may give the appearance of being well on his way to maturity—but that's far from the facts. For one thing the dog's twenty-eight milk teeth are slowly being replaced by the forty-two permanent ones. A youngster between four and seven months is in an intermittent state of teething. This can be a painful process involving diarrhea, poor appetite, depression, listlessness, and an intense desire to chew. When a young dog is teething, he is invariably going to ease the pain by chewing on objects around the house. Easing the discomfort is accomplished by providing suitable chew toys made of digestible materials, ice cubes, or a moistened—then frozen—washcloth to help ease the pain. Never give a puppy a chew toy that resembles a real object that you would not want him to chew. Old shoes and socks have the same bad effect. They teach the puppy to chew those items later, as a grown dog.

The price of a pure bred puppy and all the new equipment and services can melt your credit card and make you the plaything of your bank for thirty-six months at double digit interest. For all the wonderful reasons people buy dogs (and there are many) the cost does not seem outrageous until the young pet eats half of an orthopedic mattress and chews to pieces a digital clock radio. By the time young Lochinvar destroys a year's supply of panty hose and those new pumps from Bonwit's not even the children can save him from the headsman. But when he hops into your lap and curls up against your chest and you feel the warm flow of his puppy pulse, your emotions change and the loving glow reminds you why you got him in the first place. You look at the plush arm of your mocha-colored, suede couch and think, "No, he wouldn't. Not my beloved couch." But in your heart you know he would.

Destructive dogs are hard to cope with because we come to love them before we understand their terrible potential. Of course a continual assault on your possessions will take some of the bloom off those tender feelings and allow a thought or two about adoption

You look at the plush arm of your mocha-colored, suede couch and think, 'No, he wouldn't. Not my beloved couch.' But in your heart you know he would.

Photos, M. Siegal

agencies and a new home on a farm. But before you send the dog to the farm there are a couple of things worth trying, if only to protect your own feelings of guilt and the awful fate awaiting a disinherited house dog.

Unless your dog is a pathological chewer (and few are) he may simply be easing the pain in his gums caused by teething. If that's the case the problem will soon end. Try not to think of your dog as a Dead End Kid but, rather, as an uneducated youth with all of the problems connected with canine adolescence.

Dogs do their worst damage if they are bored; if they are lonely; if, somehow, you are the cause of frustration. These are all solvable problems and the most common, practical solution is obedience training. You may hire a professional trainer to come to your home or take the uneducated cur to a training class. You may purchase a do-it-yourself dog training book and accomplish the task on your own. There is a unique solution to the problem of boredom, loneliness or frustration which causes destructive behavior. You may get your pet a pet of his own.

Naturally, more exercise and many hours of daily companionship would be the best way to combat your dog's boredom and loneliness. A happy, busy dog rarely eats his home. But you cannot quit your job. Getting your dog a puppy or kitten to keep him company may be the next best thing. Bear in mind that dogs, like wolves, are highly social creatures who live in a *pack* society when in their natural state.

All dogs (and wolves) are social creatures by instinct. The *pack* is essentially a small family of canines living together in various states of harmony, sharing the burdens and responsibilities. If your dog is left alone much of the time, as many dogs are, he is living out the life of the *lone wolf*. It is unnatural and in some cases debilitating to his physical and mental state. A lone wolf is one who has become too old or too sick to fulfill his or her destiny within the pack order. He becomes an outcast and does not survive for very long in the wilderness. Our pet dogs understand this instinctively and may experience anxiety every time their human family leaves them alone. Leaving your dog in the company of another animal makes a great deal of sense, from the dog's point of view.

It is not suggested that your dog feed, bathe and walk his very own poochie—although, in the wild, dogs take very good care of their own. If your dog had a puppy or kitten to relate to he or she would feel more like the leader of a pack and become too busy and preoccupied with his or her ward to indulge in such foolishness as eating the baseboards off the walls.

One must be sensible, however, when taking in a second pet. Consider whether two dogs of the same or different sex would be best for you. Many consider a male and a female dog the best team. Most terriers and hunting breeds should not be given baby animals, especially if they resemble rodents in any way. Do not bring home a kitten to a dog that is a confirmed cat hater.

Always bear in mind that the dog who claimed you and your home first should get the most consideration and attention. Allow the new addition to be the possession of your older pet. The two of them will work out their own relationship to their mutual satisfaction. If all goes well the destruction of your home should stop.

It is not cruel to keep large dogs in the city providing their needs are satisfied. Nor is it cruel to leave dogs alone in an apartment for reasonable periods of time. Cruelty is not the issue on these points. Neglect and ignorance is the issue.

Although several of the larger breeds of dog are best served out of the cramped city lifestyle it is not cruel at all. Dogs are perhaps the most adaptable creatures in the animal kingdom and with proper care and intelligence on the part of the human family they can thrive in most environments. Almost all dog breeds have been deliberately contrived by humans through breeding selection for one purpose or another. Therefore they do not really have a habitat that they have evolved in through the process of *natural selection* such as the wolf or coyote. Dogs have always existed in partnership with humans and depend on them for everything. Naturally an Irish Wolfhound (or other oversized breed) would appreciate a countryside to run in, but this is hardly available anywhere. Few rural areas offer free-running space that isn't fenced off or inaccessible for one reason or another. But this can be compensated for with an intelligent exercise regimen. Long walks, vigorous play and perhaps some jogging are all valuable exercises for a city dog.

As previously stated, boredom and anxiety are the principal reasons for destruction in the home. It is not cruel to leave a dog alone for a moderate period of time. Although some dogs obsessively crave the company of their owners, most adjust to being alone from one to eight hours, depending on the dog and whether or not it had been accustomed to this from puppyhood. Puppies must be trained to be alone through a gradual process with the help of a small room or a dog crate which is simply a large, wire enclosure with a door. It serves as a comfortable, safe den or haven allowing the animal to feel that it is in its own lair. As the dog grows into adolescence it needs a larger space with nothing in it that can be chewed upon or destroyed. Some breeds and some dogs within a breed cannot bear to be left alone at all. Among such breeds are the Siberian Husky, Alaskan Malamute and Afghan Hound, so keep this in mind if you like these breeds but are not a homebody.

Once the teething period is over, and if the dog is obedience trained, *any* dog can be taught to adjust to the human family's working and social schedules.

The Swedens might have been well advised to first take Jughead out for at least one half hour's worth of exercise before leaving him alone for the evening. This would have helped him work off some of his pent-up energy. Then a short play period would have been useful in satisfying his urge to chew. The single most important thing they could have done was to confine Jughead to the kitchen, after having removed all objects within reach including the power cords of appliances. They should have left him with his chew toys, his food, and his water. If the dog was teething, a dish of ice cubes would have been beneficial. Leaving the light on and playing a radio turned to an all-news station where the dog would hear a human voice for most of the evening helps. Had these things been done, the precious carpet, sofa, and porcelain lamp would have been found later that night as they had been left. Dogs—especially puppies and adolescents—have great needs, and they must be recognized and dealt with. The alternative is too awful to consider.

2

Lean, Svelte and Portly . . . Not a Law Firm (Food)

YOUR DOG thinks that eating is his job. If he is a normal, untroubled pet, he will eat your sweat socks if you cook them in gravy. Turning your kitchen into a fast-food operation for dogs is a great temptation when you consider the convenience of opening a can of this, a bag of that, and a pot-and-plate scraping of whatever. Emptying your refrigerator of last week's chicken wings and creamed spinach into the canine bowleroo only seems economical. Actually, a dog's nutritional needs are very different from human needs and should be dealt with accordingly. Although you'll get much disagreement from your dog, the point to feeding is to have the digestive system break the food down into nutrients so that the blood can distribute them to the body for growth and fuel. Pleasure and the many weird forms of gratification from eating are human traits not truly shared by animals. Our pets, if not made crazy by us, eat only to survive. If they are not fed properly, they become vulnerable to a host of illnesses and live shorter lives.

The three sins of dog nutrition are too little, too much, and poorly balanced food. For full growth and proper functioning of all systems of the body, a dog requires a balance of protein, carbohydrate, fat, vitamins, and minerals. In the wild, this balance is achieved by capturing and devouring another animal. The first part of the downed prey that is consumed is the contents of the stomach which provides grains and/or vegetation. The flesh, the layered fat, and even the bones all contribute to the proper balance of protein, carbohydrate, and all the rest.

The dog's closest relative, the wolf, doesn't eat every day, especially during the long, hard winter months. Locating the prey and then downing it require a great deal of energy and exercise. When you couple this with the demands made on the body by the exposure to outdoor weather conditions, it is easy to calculate that the wolf or wild dog expends almost as much energy to work for his food as the energy equivalent consumed from the meal itself. One rarely comes across a fat wolf. Overfed or poorly fed domestic dogs lead shorter, unhealthier, and unhappier lives that those fed a well-rounded maintenance diet.

Among higher elevations in San Francisco is Telegraph Hill, where the fog is viewed below and the sun above. All of San Francisco can be seen from its hilly turrets. Near the top was a fine house partially hidden behind walls of shrubbery. A billowing bay window faced all of the city below and part of the winding street twisting close to the top. A constant fixture staring out at the breathtaking view from the window was a young dog named Antony.

He was the picture of indifference as the occasional Gray Line tour bus rounded the curve with its little windows filled with waving passengers. Antony always sat upon a red velour cushion tucked neatly inside a luxurious wicker bed. His throat was encircled with thick antelope hide hooked together with a silver buckle. His name was etched on a platinum tag studded with four diamond chips that dangled from his soft leather collar. Antony was part beagle and part scottie. He was an honored member of the Carmody family. Mr. Carmody was on the board of directors of a major West Coast bank, and Mrs. Carmody was the driving force of Bay Area charities, not the least of which was the SPCA, Antony's last known residence.

The sensitive, vulnerable Mrs. Carmody found the peculiar-looking dog one day while inspecting the euthanasia chamber. He just seemed too wonderfully ugly to have put down. It was love at first sight, quite luckily for the condemned dog. The society matron took the unfortunate creature to her home on Telegraph Hill and named him Antony. She lavished him in luxuries few dogs ever enjoy. Her attachment to Antony was swift and total. The dog's reserved demeanor proclaimed just the proper amount of aloof dignity that she admired the most. Charles Carmody understood very quickly that his wife Patricia adored her new dog. He never fully understood why she loved this funny little mutt when she could have had the most expensive specimen of any breed in the world, one with an outstanding pedigree. But Antony was all she ever wanted in a dog.

The rich young dog hardly moved from his cushion all day and was brought his meals in porcelain bowls as he continually stared out the window. The food was prepared by Mrs. Carmody's housekeeper and constant companion and friend, Aleta Barnes. As the elderly Miss Barnes adored her friend and employer, she also came to adore the standoffish dog with the distant gaze. Her personal concern for the dog was reflected in all her efforts for the animal's safety and well-being.

Antony was offered the finest cuts of prime beef and milky veal, not to mention broiled hen and dazzling omelets. At first the meals were discreetly placed next to his wicker lounge. He nibbled halfway through and left the rest. As time progressed, he left more than he ate. Miss Barnes then tried feeding the dog directly with the help of pewter tongs. Antony turned his face away with a hurt expression. Finally, Mrs. Carmody herself, with great worry, began offering small silver forkfuls with baby-talk entreaties. With soulful eyes, Antony would take four bites of food but no more, and that was merely a token of his esteem and appreciation for the good woman. Antony was just not hungry—or something.

Mrs. Carmody giggled and confided that she admired his finicky attitude. She felt it was more the discernment of an epicure who was used to better fare than was being offered. She told Miss Barnes that she herself had never eaten a restaurant meal that she finished and almost never touched the food at a dinner party. "Nobody cooks decent food anymore," she proclaimed in defense of the abstaining little dog. "If he could only speak, the poor dear, I'd ask him to supervise his own menu or at least select a chef of his own choosing." Miss Barnes shook her head with amusement. But Antony gazed deep into their faces as though trying to say something important. The futility of it all just caused him to sigh deeply in endured frustration as he turned once again to stare out at the city below.

"Nobody cooks decent food anymore," she proclaimed
in defense of the abstaining little dog.   *Dan Farrell*

It was Aleta Barnes who noticed the dog's loss of weight. She had a difficult time of it trying to convince Mrs. Carmody that Antony's rejection of food could indicate that he needed a veterinarian rather than a new chef. Even the most discriminating dog has to eat something every day. Mrs. Carmody halfheartedly conceded the point. "I'd rather he were finicky than sick. Call Dr. What's-his-name at the shelter. God, he has cold fingers." Miss Barnes smiled victoriously.

The chief veterinarian of the SPCA was summoned to the Carmody household to examine the dog. After a brief examination, he gave the dog a clean bill of health. The old vet did caution Mrs. Carmody that if Antony's poor eating performance continued, nothing could prevent the dog from coming down with something serious. It was suggested that the forlorn animal be force-fed for his own good. The idea of force-feeding Antony was so obnoxious to Mrs. Carmody that she seriously considered having the good doctor replaced at the clinic, cold fingers and all.

"But Mrs. Carmody, what are we going to do about Antony?" asked a worried Miss Barnes.

"Do? I'll tell you what we're going to do," replied the exasperated woman. "We're going to find the most important veterinarian in the country and have *him* figure it out."

A doctor of veterinary medicine was found in a midwestern university. Many professionals considered him the most important man in small-animal medicine. Pressure was brought to bear, and he was flown to San Francisco for Antony's sake.

Although the high fee and the expense-paid trip to San Francisco were attractive, it was hard for Dr. Triling Mansfield to take Mrs. Carmody and her problem very seriously. It wasn't until she offered to build him a new research laboratory that he took Antony's problem to heart. As a matter of fact, Dr. Mansfield assured his future benefactor that the problem could be solved very soon and that he was the one to solve it.

In two weeks between fantasies of groundbreaking ceremonies and ribbon-cutting celebrations, Dr. Mansfield tried every technique in his magical black bag to get Antony to eat. He started with a complete medical workup, including blood and stool analysis, X rays, electrocardiograms, electroencephalograms, and a complete check of the central nervous system. Having determined that there was absolutely no sign of disease, the ambitious doctor administered vitam B^{12} injections along with other appetite stimulants. Nothing. He changed the flora in the dog's intestines. Antony continued to lose weight. The frustrated veterinarian tried various diets including one that involved brown rice and poached pork fat. It offended the shaggy little dog. He was offered everything from boiled tripe soaked in yeast and desiccated liver to strawberry yogurt and meatball pizza. Antony would sigh and turn away. With visions of his newly appointed laboratory blowing away like a crumbled sheet of paper, Dr. Mansfield began to panic.

With the help of a San Francisco colleague whom he offered a post in his facility (when built), he began acupuncture treatments. It was all to no avail. Antony was in a deep state of ennui and just couldn't respond to the slender needles and burning herbs. If they could only understand his sorrowful gaze they'd know everything. Mansfield did everything but a rain dance to induce the dog to eat but he failed.

There was one final procedure that Mansfield wanted to try, but it required the sophisticated equipment available only at Stanford University's School of Veterinary Medicine. With Mrs. Carmody's permission, he placed the dog on a leash and took him outside. They started for his car when Antony caught the doctor by surprise and bolted for his freedom. Mansfield made a frantic effort to recover the dog. The animal was just too fast for a man of his advancing years. With pale gums and trembling hands, the ashen-faced doctor had to report the loss to Mrs. Carmody, who promised him his rewards in another life. Mansfield left the state with Mrs. Carmody's threat still ringing in his ears about never setting foot on California soil again.

The days turned into weeks, and there was no sign or word of Mrs. Carmody's precious pet. She and Miss Barnes both grieved and were of a mind to consider the little dog dead from malnutrition. Tears fell on Telegraph Hill, and a state of mourning fell over the grand house. Mr. Carmody decided it was time for his wife to let go of the past, so he took her on a Mediterranean cruise. He hoped she would soon recover from the wrenching experience.

The bereaved couple were at sea for three days when a call was received at their house. Miss Barnes clutched at her heart when the voice on the phone said he wanted to return a diamond ID tag and silver-buckled collar. In a flurry of pencil, paper, and stuttering emotion, she scribbled down an address and said she would be there

Photos by M. Siegal

directly. The man had introduced himself as Captain Jose Varagas and had told her to appear at the end of Fisherman's Wharf and to look for the vessel *Marcello IV.*

Miss Barnes never noticed the enticing smell of cooked shrimp and crabs or the large throngs of people milling about purchasing clams-on-the-halfshell and gaudy seashells with purple feathers protruding from them. She frantically searched for and found the *Marcello IV,* a scroungy commercial fishing boat approximately fifty feet in length and in desperate need of a barnacle scraping. Waiting on the dock was Varagas, an older man with a very gruff manner and the thickest, blackest moustache in California. Trying to avoid contaminating her dress with the smell of raw fish, Miss Barnes introduced herself and asked to see the dog. The captain informed her that he was the dog's original owner until his boat sailed by accident without little "Escudo." In his old life, Antony worked on the *Marcello IV* as part of the crew. He was a veteran of twelve voyages and earned his keep like everyone else.

The two parties explained their respective interests in the dog and tried to make their positions understood. Aleta Barnes was quite prepared to take the little dog home, but Varagas pointed out that he was already home and should be permitted to stay there. He said that the only reason he called was the obvious value of the dog's collar and tag. An argument ensued over the dog's ownership. Both captain and housekeeper flared in anger. Threats were made. With the full weight of the Carmody stature behind her, she threatened to make more trouble for the captain than he ever dreamed of, from Coast Guard scrutiny to municipal inspections.

Suddenly she heard the dog barking from below the boat. He unexpectedly appeared on the top of the net full of freshly caught fish as it was being hoisted from the hold to the large receiving bins on the dock. The dog was dark with slick grime and fish blood. His fur was matted from the sticky fish, saltwater, and seaweed. He was not exactly the Antony Aleta Barnes knew who sat on his red cushion atop Telegraph Hill. However, the dog had gained close to six pounds and looked as solid as a potroast. His eyes were bright and his body moved with excitement and energy.

When she recovered from her amazement, Miss Barnes asked the captain what they had been feeding Antony—"Ah, I mean Escudo."

"Dog food," he replied. "Only the best, though. He's a funny dog. He only eats when he's happy and working makes him happy. Look, he's gonna get his favorite food now because he worked very hard on this voyage."

The first mate called Escudo over to him in Portuguese and made the dog jump for his coveted treat. It was a large fish head severed from an eleven-pound bonito. As the dog went to work on the unhappy object, Miss Barnes tried not to be disgusted as she sighed with resignation. She then made a decision that could get her into a lot of trouble with the quick-tempered Patricia Carmody.

"Captain Varagas," she proclaimed, "I want you to take the collar and ID tag and drop them in the ocean the next time out. Will you do that for me?"

Varagas understood and nodded solemnly. Suppressing her sadness halfway down and twisting it into a knot, she added, "Give Escudo another one of those—things, you know, heads, for me and treat him well. He is a magnificent dog, you know." The captain agreed. "By the way, what does Escudo mean?"

The captain smiled revealing two gold teeth toward the back of his mouth. "Oh, it is Portuguese for one dollar. That's how much I paid for him."

She smiled and left the dock but turned back because it occurred to her that Escudo never once acknowledged her presence or even noticed her for that matter. She waved good-bye as the little dog took an indelicate bite dangerously close to one fish eye.

"Good-bye, Antony," she whispered with more than a little hurt.

One could hardly accuse Antony of being a finicky eater. His staple diet consisted of commercial dog food and an occasional fish head. It was the loss of his old life that took him off his feed. He would rather have gone into the euthanasia chamber at the SPCA than live away from his master, his fishing boat, and the other people in his life. The rich gourmet foods prepared for him daily had no meaning or value to him as a dog and were a complete waste of time. He probably would have refused to eat his normal diet even if the Carmodys knew what it was. Antony wanted to be Escudo once again and feel the deck of the boat under his paws as they headed toward deep waters. He wanted the life they had given him since puppyhood. There is a large difference between a dog off his feed and one that is considered "finicky."

A dog that insists on one type of food over another is usually involved in some neurotic game created and encouraged by a human. When a very young dog enters a human situation, it takes on many of the behavioral aspects of the environment, and that includes neurotic game-playing. When the finicky dog is fed along the lines of taste preference (the human's concept of the dog's taste preference, that is), then he learns to manipulate human behavior by eating or not eating. Some finicky dogs have been programmed to expect an elaborate set of food and feeding conditions, and if his owner forgets just one element of the pattern the dog refuses to eat.

Clearly this type of dog has been drawn into a neurotic situation which can only distort the true nature of the animal. However, it is safe to say that domestication itself is a distortion of the original life-style of dogs. In the wild, like wolves, they are drawn into packs. They must forage for food or strenuously hunt for sick or young herding animals. This means they they do not necessarily eat every day, nor does every member of the pack eat equally well. When a large game animal is brought down, the pack leader is the first to eat and takes the largest, choicest portions. But there is a natural logic to this behavior. The lead male wolf or wild dog returns to the den and disgorges a large quantity of undigested food for the lactating female and/or weaning puppies. Harder work and greater responsibility require more nutritional intake.

Domestically, however, dogs are not the leaders of their packs, nor should they be. A domestic dog is the one that is fed at the sufferance of the human caretaker who is, in effect, the pack leader. Domestic dogs that dictate the terms of their feeding habits are behaving in an unnatural manner considering their position in the pack (human family).

From September to March, wild canids are nomadic and follow the grazing herds as a source of food. Between April and August, they remain within the boundaries of a fixed territory and eat squirrels, rabbits, small rodents, birds, fish, berries, and small fruits. Food is never more than a means to satisfying nutritional needs within the body. It has nothing to do with pleasure (in human terms), culinary art, aesthetics, or any of the social graces. Further, in the wild, food has no emotional or psychological meaning. It does not relate to love, acceptance, guilt, emotional stability, sexual behavior, or dependencies brought about through bribery or blackmail. These are neurotic values given to food by human beings. Unfortunately, some domestic dogs are taught to respond to them by their human families. This represents a clash between the animal's natural feeding instincts and conditions imposed on dogs by their human owners. This can lead only to bad behavior such as growling and biting over food; finicky behavior; withholding affection (gourmandise blackmail).

Too many pet owners feed their dogs as a means of soliciting their love and attention. Food is not love! Nor is it the currency of love. Allowing a bit of philosophy, love is an emotion requiring no qualifications or payments. It is either present or not. Heaping a dog's bowl with leftover roast beef, mashed potatoes, carrots, gravy and fat trimmings does not mean that you and your dog should buy furniture and take an apartment together. It merely makes the animal a four-legged garbage can of a love object. Dog owners must be able to separate their own relationship with food from their dogs'. Dogs eat to live and not the other way around.

Obviously, feeding a dog involves finding the most nutritional food available (a high-quality commercial food) and making no big fuss over its presentation. The same applies if the dog is fed a home-cooked diet with vitamin supplements.

Dogs that will not eat at all are usually suffering from a physical ailment. There are those dogs, however, that go off their feed because of an emotional problem. Such was the case of Antony or Escudo. All that was important to the little dog was lost including his owner, his environment, his established diet, and, most important of all, his job. The most luxurious life in the world could not compensate for what was existentially the only true reality the dog knew. Many animals, including humans, pack animals and herding animals, will die in the face of plenty if they lose their positions in their respective societies. There is strong evidence that all animals are either given or develop a role for themselves in their social frameworks. When an animal is denied that role because of failing health, defeat, or alienation, he becomes a self-sentenced "lone wolf." This isolated creature wanders off in a meaningless journey from which there is no returning. Allowing a loved pet to eat like a dog rather than a human is probably more valuable to the animal's health than the composition of the food itself.

The other side of the same coin is when the family pet begins to resemble a teenage Volkswagen. Warfare ensues in the kitchen. When a dog is loved to an extreme degree by its human owner it is often attacked daily with a deadly barrage of guided missiles fired off from the refrigerator. In such cases the kitchen is the battlefield and eventually becomes the killing ground because obesity in dogs and humans has the same lethal effect. It gradually destroys good health. Obesity shortens the life span of an animal and louses up the quality of life as well.

And please do not stub your toe by saying *My dog isn't obese, he's merely big-boned and filled out.* Medically speaking, your pet does not have to resemble the Goodyear blimp to qualify. If a dog is 15 to 20 percent overweight he is obese.

It is quite true that some members of a breed are simply larger specimens than others. Therefore, one must learn how to determine when a dog is carrying too much weight. Obviously, an obese dog is easily identified like white socks with a tuxedo. They tend to stand out from the crowd. Detecting the overweight dog requires a few guidelines.

Merely weighing the dog is not much help unless a veterinarian has already determined your pet's ideal weight range. If that is the case, then you should weigh your fat dog once a week. This is not very difficult. With most breeds this can be done by subtracting your own weight from the combined weight of you and your dog when you're both on the scale.

Each canine is different physically and does have variables that must be taken into account. These variables have to do with breed of dog, bone structure, sex, working conditions, living conditions, weather conditions and other environmental factors. These all help determine what the ideal weight for your dog should be. Young dogs are still growing while old dogs are just getting heavier. Dogs that work for a living or who live in outdoor kennels all year require anywhere from 10% to 100% more calories than sedentary dogs living indoors. The female of a breed, as a rule, is somewhat smaller in bone structure and therefore should be fed a little less than her male counterpart. Dogs who are outdoors in cold weather will eat more than those who almost never get out.

On a general basis here are a few guides for ideal weight by breed and size. Very small breeds such as Chihuahuas, Pekingese, Miniature Schnauzers should weigh between 4 and 15 pounds. Of the small breeds the Boston Terriers and Cocker Spaniels should weigh between 19 and 25 pounds. Of the medium breeds the Beagles, Brittany Spaniels and Siberian Huskies should weigh between 30 and 55 pounds. In the large breed category the Airedales, 50 pounds; Standard Poodle, 55; Pointer, 65; Golden Retriever, 70; Labrador Retriever, 70 pounds. The *very* large breeds weigh considerably more. Old English Sheepdogs should weigh approximately 95 pounds; Great Pyrenees, 115; Great Danes, 130; Newfoundlands, 140; St. Bernards, 165.

For most dogs, obesity starts in puppyhood with little or no knowledge of nutrition on the part of the owner. The entire situation can be summed up in one word: *overfeeding.* If a puppy or young dog is fed table scraps, then the quantity of food he eats depends on the human appetite and how much has gone uneaten at the dinner table.

Look your Big Daddy over and watch for visible fat protrusions such as a hanging stomach, double and triple chins, loose flesh around the collar or a shapeless torso that is one solid cylinder shape from neck to tail. If any or all of these conditions exist we're talking fat.

One excellent technique for a fat alert is to check what's happening around the animal's rib cage. Feel around the underside of your dog's trunk, his chest. Run your palm along the ribs on each side of the cage. A healthy, normal dog does not have too much tissue between the skin and the ribs. It is easy to feel each and every rib on a dog of normal weight. There should be just enough tissue to make a slight finger indentation when pressed against the rib, no more. To be precise, one fifth of an inch of tissue covering the ribs is the acceptable amount. Anything more than this indicates an overweight dog. This is especially true when the ribs cannot be felt or seen in outline form. Look out, make way for a fatso dog.

Obesity is almost always a feeding problem created so long ago when the old dog was just a cute little muff of a pup. Let's face it, fat comes from eating more calories than one burns off during the course of a normal day's routine of physical and mental activity. Because the first year for a dog is one of intense growth the novice dog owner witnesses the animal devouring every morsel available. This is misinterpreted as a permanent way of feeding. In addition, food is offered as a reward, as a symbol of love, of affection, of acceptance, of happiness. For these unfortunate animals food becomes something

"If over-fed and under-exercised this snoozing pooch will eventually need a diet or a veterinarian or both." *Gaines*

beyond nutritional fuel for the body's needs. Eating turns into a habit, an obsession, an addiction.

It is worth mentioning that studies of obese dogs made by veterinary researchers found that no less than 44% of the obese dogs observed were owned by obese humans.

There are several options for reducing your dog's weight. First, you can simply reduce your dog's diet by 40, 50 or even 60%. Many veterinarians will suggest this. Second, there are several commercially prepared food products designed to feed the dog with fewer calories. These are excellent products and do help satisfy your dog's appetite while reducing his caloric intake.

People who overfeed their dogs or indulge them in exotic cookery do so out of deep feelings for their animals. They are like loving, doting parents who make many mistakes. A misuse of the meaning of love is often manifested in fat dogs, fat children and fat spouses. Of course, there are many other reasons why dogs get fat but they are all related to overeating, or rather, over-feeding. A human cooks his own goose but a dog has to have it done for him. Repeat after me: FOOD IS NOT LOVE. Again.

The nutritional requirements of dogs have been scientifically determined as a general set of principles. Each dog's body chemistry, however, is different and therefore uses nutritional intake in its own unique manner and style. However, enough is known to give every dog owner the knowledge to sufficiently feed every dog under most circumstances allowing for the necessary adjustments for individual dogs. Here, then, is a scientific compromise for feeding dogs made necessary by domestication.

According to Mark L. Morris, Jr., D.V.M., Ph.D., one of the nation's leading animal nutritionists and director of Mark Morris Associates of Topeka, Kansas, feeding a dog commercially prepared food is fine, but figuring out the exact quantity to give can be elusive and complicated. He cites the example of two laboratory Beagles the same size, height, and weight. One dog can eat 20 calories per pound of body weight and get fat, while the other may eat 37 calories per pound of body weight and remain slim. In other words, the caloric requirements differ from dog to dog, and that may simply relate to the peculiarities of a given dog's body chemistry—let alone his environment, state of health, or activity.

Dr. Morris recommends that the dog owner make an eyeball judgment as to what is the optimum body weight for his or her animal.

Use the following general feeding formula and weigh the dog once a week to determine if weight is gained, lost, or maintained; then adjust the food amount according to the dog's need to gain, lose, or maintain weight. Prescribed amounts of commercial dog food based on quantities are not accurate unless you know the calorie count of the food involved in terms of a measured quantity. Canned dog foods vary in caloric count from 400 calories per can to 650 and 700 calories per can. Dry food will also vary, but within a narrower range: from 1,500 calories to 2,000 calories per pound. When you convert calories to measured cups, you must do it on the basis of the caloric count of the individual product, and that information is not always on the label.

When deciding how much to feed your dog, consider:

One can of average dog food will feed approximately 20 pounds of dog per day (based on 500 or 550 calories per 20 pounds).

One pound of dry food will feed approximately 60 to 65 pounds of dog per day. Five ounces of dry food will feed about 20 pounds of dog per day.

One patty of soft-moist (burger type) is approximately equal to ½ can of dog food. One packet will equal approximately 1 can of dog food. Thus, one patty will feed approximately 10 pounds of dog per day.

But dogs live different life-styles and are often in varied states of health. In the winter, an outdoor dog's caloric requirements may increase by as much as 40 percent. When feeding puppies, according to Dr. Morris, allow them to eat as much as they want during the growth period (from weaning to six or eight months, and in larger breeds, even longer). This is called ad libitum, or self-feeding. Always replenish the puppy's food bowl when it is empty. (Dry food and supplements are the most practical type for this plan.) A pregnant bitch should be fed her normal maintenance diet until the end of the sixth week of gestation. During the last three weeks, food must be increased by approximately 25 or 30 percent. During the six weeks of lactation she may increase her food intake by almost three times her normal maintenance quantity. This quantity must be made available for the proper maintenance of good health.

Refer to the following nutritional charts for further understanding of your dog's feeding requirements. It is always best to consult your veterinarian for definitive information regarding your dog's individual needs.

Feeding a dog a proper diet, one that maintains the animal without producing excessive weight gain or loss, is probably the most important kindness a human can give to that pet. Good nutrition promises long life, good health, and a happy relationship.

Guide for Caloric Requirements of the Dog During the Life Cycle

| | Required Calories/lb. Body Weight/24 Hours | | |
	(15 lb. & under)*	(20-50 lb.)*	(60-100 lb.)*
LIFE STAGE			
Maintenance	40	30	25
Growth			
6 weeks	120	150	150
8 weeks	100	130	100
3 months	90	90	75
6 months	60	60	60
Lactation			
1 week	76	60	52
2 weeks	95	75	65
3 weeks	105	81	71
4 weeks	114	90	76
5 weeks	112	103	105
6 weeks	88	79	89
7 weeks	48	40	60

*Mature weight.

Vitamin Requirements and Their Deficiency Signs in the Dog

Vitamin	Recommended Daily Dietary Level/kg. Body Weight Growth	Maintenance	Main Deficiency Sign	Sources	Signs of Hypervitamin<
A	200 I.U.	100 I.U.	Poor growth, xerophthalmia, suppurative skin disease, impaired bone growth.	Fish oils, corn, egg yolk, liver.	Seen more frequently than deficiency. Anorexia, weight loss, decalcification of bone hypersthesia, joint ill.
D	10 I.U. (Assumes a 1.2:1 calcium:phosphorus ratio)	7 I.U.	Rickets in young and osteomalacia in adults Also lordosis, chest deformity and poor eruption of permanent teeth.	Sunlight, irradiated yeast, fish liver oils, egg yolk.	Seen more frequently than deficiency. Anorexia, nausea, fatigue, renal damage, soft tissue calcification hypercalemia, diarrhea dehydration, death.
E	2.2 mg. (Depends upon level of unsaturated fat in the ration)	2.2 mg.	Reproductive failure with weal or dead feti. Nutritional muscular dystrophy, steatitis.	Egg yolk, corn, milk fat, cereal germs.	None recorded.
K	Not required except during antibacterial therapy or chronic intestinal diseases		Impaired prothrombin formation, hence reduced clotting time and hemorrhage.	Yeast, liver, fish meal, soybeans.	None recorded but hig levels probably dangerous.
C	Not a dietary requirement in normal dogs		Retarded healing, increased susceptibility to disease.	Fresh fruits and vegetables, canned orange juice contains about 0.5 mg/ml.	Nontoxic.
Thiamine	36 mcgs.	18 mcgs.	Anorexia, arrested growth, muscular weakness, ataxia.	Yeast, liver, whole grains.	No toxic effect with moderate overdosage.
Riboflavin	.08 mg.	.04 mg.	Dry scaly skin, erythema of hind legs and chest, muscular weakness in hing quarters, anemia, sudden death.	Milk, yeast and whole grains; dextrin, cornstarch favor synthesis.	Nontoxic even in large amounts.

Vitamin	Recommended Daily Dietary Level/kg. Body Weight Growth	Maintenance	Main Deficiency Sign	Sources	Signs of Hypervitaminosis
Niacin	400 mcgs.	220 mcgs.	"Black tongue," i.e., anorexia, weight loss, diarrhea, anemia, reddening and ulceration of mucous membranes of mouth and tongue, death.	Whole grains, yeast, meat, scraps, tankage, fish meal, eggs. Tryptophan for synthesis.	Dilation of blood vessels, itching, burning of skin.
Pyridoxine	44 mcgs.	22 mcgs.	Microcytic hypochromic anemia, high serum iron and atherosclerosis.	Whole grains, milk, meat, fish, yeast, liver.	No toxicity data has been reported.
Pantothenic Acid	200 mcgs.	50 mcgs.	Anorexia, hypoglycemia, hypochloremia, BUN increase, gastritis, enteritis, convulsions, coma and death.	Yeast, dairy products, liver, rice	No data available.
Folic Acid	8.8 mcgs.	4.4 mcgs.	Hypoplasia of bone marrow, hypochromic microcytic anemia, glossitis.	Yeast, liver.	Nontoxic.
Biotin	NONE on natural diets. Deficiency usually associated with feeding of raw eggs.		Tension, aimless wandering, spasticity of hind legs, progressive paralysis.	Liver, kidney, milk, egg yolk, yeast.	Nontoxic.
Cobalamin B$_{12}$)	1 mcg.	0.7 mcg.	Anemia	Liver, fish meal, meat scraps, dairy products.	Nontoxic.
Choline	55 mg.	—	Fatty infiltration of liver, increase in plasma, phosphatase, decrease in plasma protein, prothrombin time, hemoglobin and P.C.V. values.	Yeast, liver, meat scraps, soybean oil, egg yolk.	Persistent diarrhea caused by 10 gms/day or greater.

Mineral Requirements and Their Deficiency Signs in the Dog

Mineral	Recommended Dietary Level	Common Sources	Common Deficiency Signs
Calcium	1.0%	Steamed bone meal Dicalcium phosphate Ground green bone Ground oyster shell	Enlarged epiphysis of long bones and ribs, splaying of toes, hyperextension of the carpus and tarsus, spontaneous fractures and abnormal deviation of the legs.*
Phosphorus	0.9%	Steamed bone meal Dicalcium phosphate Ground green bone	Same as above*
Sodium Chloride	Not required as such	Table salt	Deficiency is rare. Natural feedstuffs contain adequate amounts. When the deficiency occurs, weight loss, hair loss, acidosis and eventually death may be seen.
Potassium	0.8%	Potassium chloride	Deficiency is rare. Natural feedstuffs contain adequate amounts. When the deficiency occurs, ascending paralysis, depressed reflexes may be seen.
Magnesium	0.1%	Manganese carbonate Magnesium oxide Magnesium sulfate	Retarded growth, spreading of toes and hyperextension of carpus and tarsus, hyperirritability, convulsions, soft tissue calcification, enlargement of the epiphysis of long bones.*
	mg./lb. of food		
Iron	25.0	Iron carbonate Iron sulfate	Microcytic-hypochromic anemia, anisocytosis and poikilocytosis of erythrocytes.
Manganese	2.2	Manganese oxide Manganese carbonate Manganese sulfate	Deficiency is rare. Crooked, shortened soft bones may be seen.*
Copper	3.5	Copper sulfate Copper carbonate Copper oxide	Reduction in erythrocytes, swelling of ends of long bones, hyperextension of carpus.*
Cobalt	1.0	Cobalt chloride Cobalt carbonate	Normocytic-normochromic anemia.
Zinc	2.2	Zinc oxide	Deficiency is rare. Natural feedstuffs contain adequate amounts except when extreme calcium supplementation is attempted by overzealous dog owners.
Iodine	0.7	Iodized salt Sodium iodide Potassium iodide	Dead or goitrous pups. Erythematous dermatitis.

*Deficiency signs of calcium, phosphorus, vitamin D, magnesium, manganese or copper deficiency may be difficult or impossible to differentiate clinically.

3

A Guide for Housebreakers

Toileting

"Housebreaking" is one of those words like "prunes"—it always gets a laugh, or at least a silly smirk. Housebreaking never gets a laugh from a novice dog owner with a seven-month-old Alaskan Malamute who leaves calling cards all over the house. Housebreaking also gets few laughs from the owner of the toy dog who dumps in the middle of the bed at the Holiday Inn.

Like pregnancy, a dog is never partially housebroken. "In for a dime in for a dollar." It is of no use to a dog owner to have an animal reliable for seven days in a row and then have to step in something left behind on the eighth. Unless the animal is sick, there is no reason to tolerate an unhousebroken dog.

From your dog's point of view, the elimination of body waste is just about the least important reason to urinate and defecate. These functions comprise the most effective means of communication (with other dogs, primarily) nature has provided. Although a dog possesses keen vision, his sense of smell is even better. When one dog urinates or defecates in a particular locale, sooner or later all other dogs in the area become aware of it no matter how long the material has been sitting there. A dog's nose is his most efficient mechanism. He can smell better than humans and can discern and file away in his memory over ten thousand separate and distinct odors.

Dogs proclaim for all others in the area, "I am here" whenever they eliminate in a city street or on a country bush. Sometimes it is an effort to communicate with their human family if they are lost. In the wild, territory is marked off with this scent-posting technique, and members of the same pack know the parameters of their pack's terrain. It is also a warning to members of other packs that this area is spoken for and is a guide to proper pack identification. The hunting range for wolves changes with the migration of prey animals and is determined in part by weather conditions and food availability. Therefore, scent-posting is a continuing activity as the pack moves from terrain to terrain.

We must view the domestic dog's eliminative behavior with this in mind. Just like wolves, pet dogs continue to mark their imagined territory with urine and droppings. They no longer know why they do it, but some vestigial wire continues to function in an abandoned printed circuit in the lost passageways of the brain. Like a message in a bottle or light traveling from a star, a dog's eliminations send out personal information to others passing through his time and space.

Sex is another important factor involved in the elimination of urine and fecal matter. When a female is in heat, she produces a strong odor that is present in the waste matter. It is yet another technique of communicating the fact that a female in the territory is in season and ready to mate. Male dogs are magnetically drawn to this odor and attempt to find nature's temptress. When it comes to housebreaking problems for dog owners, there is more to it than meets the eye.

Harold Greer gave his wife Doris a Yorkshire Terrier puppy for her twenty-eighth birthday. He had gone to a great deal of trouble, and he made the purchase with the help of a list of breeders supplied by the American Kennel Club. Doris cooed with pleasure as she clutched the tiny canine and in an instant named him Pudding. He peed all over her blouse.

Newspapers were spread out on a portion of the kitchen floor and all manner of sign language and primitive grunts were tried in order to communicate what they wanted from the small dog. It was always too late by the time the papers were spread out. They'd place the small animal on the Sunday magazine and tell Pudding to wee-wee, to pee-pee, to make, to go, to give mommy her jewels, to let it all hang out, to make plop-plops, to move, to try, to crappy and, finally, to drop dead. To their complete and utter frustration, Pudding always seemed to wait until he was allowed into the living room before letting loose.

Mr. Greer sold diamonds at Cartier's and was accustomed to a muted, dignified existence. But even this subdued gentleman lost his composure and began quietly stepping on Pudding's paws behind Mrs. Greer's back. It was clearly an act of retaliation. He once raised his hand to slap the misbehaving dog, but his wife shrieked in horror. His flattened hand turned knuckle-white and throbbed as it sought a place to hide. In the beginning the little dog eagerly waited for his owners to see his little beads of waste matter and to receive their applause. It soon became apparent that these people did not appreciate his minor triumphs. It was beyond his comprehension. They would yell and holler at his proud little puddles, and all he could do was cock his head to one side and try to read their lips.

Pudding did not read, write, or speak English. Nor did he fathom the peculiar attitude of humans toward fecal declarations of the existential self. His communiques in dog language were as effective as Western Union and every bit as eloquent as the Hallmark product. What was wrong? He was in a foreign country on a raincheck and was trying very hard to become streetwise, but no one knew how or what to teach him. And so, every once in a while, he knew he was going to be yelled at and punished in some way. He resigned himself to the daily unpleasantness of being a prisoner of war.

Through a process of trial and error, Pudding learned that they became less upset when he eliminated on their newspapers and absolutely ecstatic when he let go outdoors. But there was nothing definitive about the situation. The dog still found himself compelled to return to the old soiled spots on the carpet and reaffirm his presence with a declaration of assertion written in urine. It did not win him any popularity contests. From the Greers' point of view, the dog was slowly learning how to behave, possible through osmosis or

In the beginning, the little dog eagerly waited for his owners to see his little beads of waste matter and to receive their applause. *M. Siegal*

some feat of extrasensory perception. Doris Green was convinced that things were going well (a relative term in this case) because she had changed her mantra from Vishnu to Pudding.

Harold Greer was forced to give up his meditation because that was the time the dog chose to relieve himself—a sort of meditation break, as it were. The thought that Pudding was dirtying the wall-to-wall kept creeping into the eastern silence and had the opposite effect of meditation. Greer's response was far from relaxed. His legs would become prickly and restless as if the blood ceased to flow to them. They tingled like sour pickles and his palms would sweat. He hated it when his palms sweated. It reminded him of those awful moments in the upstairs salon just before an important client decided to take or leave a major purchase. Meditation was supposed to make him forget the jewelry business, but Pudding's nutritional residue began to look like necklaces and bracelets.

For days Greer tried hard to accomplish his quiet time, but he always quit early because the dog's face constantly appeared before his closed eyes like a recurring daydream. On the last day he meditated, he valiantly fought the mental picture of Pudding's mess with the word *Ahimsa,* a $100 mantra bought new. His stomach muscles tensed and beads of perspiration formed everywhere as he repeated the word over and over again. Like a child's punishment on the blackboard, he repeated the mantra quickly, then slowly, then faster and faster. By the eighth minute, foam formed at the corners of his mouth, and he was saying the word furiously until he could hear his voice ring against the walls, "AHIMSA, GOD DAMN IT!"

Mr. Greer gave up meditation about the same time that Mrs. Greer decided Pudding was housebroken because he occasionally used the newspapers. Of course that didn't change the dog's love for the carpet. He still kept his hand in, so to speak.

For several months everybody settled for the status quo. Mrs. Greer continued to refer to Pudding as a housebroken dog, and Mr. Greer spent more time at work than ever before. He often came home after his wife had retired for the evening, and he would slip carefully into the dimly lit apartment for fear of stepping on one of Pudding's quasi-housebroken manifestations. This caution was created by an unfortunate incident one evening when he came home and smeared his black patent shoes and the cuff of his gray pinstriped suit. Playing their parts, Doris pretended she was satisfied with the dog's behavior, and Harold discreetly cleaned up. Something good did come out of all this, however. Because of his long hours of overtime spent at the store which was interpreted as devotion to the firm, Cartier, Incorporated promoted Mr. Greer from engagement rings to evening jewelry. The cost of each transaction was breathtaking, and there seemed to be more dignity in dealing with lovers than suitors. It was a seller's market and an exclusive education in the law of supply and demand. It was a step up, he imagined.

The pretense over Pudding came to an abrupt ending during a shocking session in the divorce court. It seemed that from time to time Mr. Greer dipped his hand into more than the velvet necklace trays at work. He was discovered at an intimate restaurant in the company of a frequent client. Doris was passing by the neighborhood bistro and spotted Harold through the window as he was spooning out some chocolate mousse onto the plate of a mascara-eyed, stiff-sprayed blonde not quite past her prime. Doris was walking the dog who stopped directly in front of that fateful window.

Harold stuck by his story. He was working late that evening and wasn't anywhere near a restaurant. She must have mistaken him for someone else. The story didn't wash because he could not explain a dried dollop of chocolate mousse on the cuff of his jacket, his shirtsleeve, and his opal-studded cufflink.

The evidence revealed the truth, and it proved to be an open-and-shut case. All that was left was the fight over alimony and a property settlement. It wound up as a contested divorce in court. At the trial, each attorney handed the judge a list of property demands. With more than a little surprise, the judge noted that each had awarded *the other* custody of Pudding. The judge demanded to see the little dog in question and settled the matter by making Pudding a ward of the state. Off the record, the judge summarily adopted the Yorkie, took him home, and housebroke the dog himself according to the advice given in a dog-training manual.

Many months before their final decree, Harold and Doris reconciled their differences. Harold moved back into the apartment after successfully courting his wife. They lived happily ever after—with a cat.

Not everyone should own a dog. And there is no such thing as a half-housebroken dog! Either he is or he isn't. When it comes to body waste, communication is the name of the game. If the animal is not scent-posting, he is telling you something else. For example, a dog's inability to be housebroken is often a barometer of his physical or emotional well-being. A very small breed such as a Yorkshire terrier may be nervous or excitable and have a more difficult time gaining control of his bladder. Excessive wetting can also be a display of submissiveness if your dog is overwhelmed by his family or has been relegated to a subordinate position in his litter.

If a young dog or puppy has worms, and most of them get worms sooner or later, he will not be able to control his body waste. A frightened, bored, lonely, or highly nervous dog has more trouble than a dog on an even emotional keel. There is no such thing as spite in matters pertaining to housebreaking. A dog may eliminate indoors even though he is supposed to be trained not to, but it is never because of spite. To punish or spite a human is simply too sophisticated for a dog.

Sometimes the dog's indoor messing is neurotic, but not in the sense that we understand the word. Here the word "neurotic" means that which is abnormal for dog behavior, such as dirtying his own nest (living area). If a dog messes on his owner's bed, it may be a distress signal or an urgent need to scent-post. It is impossible for this to be a means of punishing a human for leaving the dog alone. Neurotic behavior in dogs is based on fear such as the fear of punishment, thunder, or being left alone. When a dog behaves neurotically, try to understand what it is that he is afraid of and change the conditions of his environment which frighten him. If this is not practical, get help from a professional dog trainer.

It is quite natural for a dog to eliminate in his own territory. Nature has set it up that way. To force a dog not to do it is to go against his nature. What is required is a means of communication to the dog that some behavior displeases you while other behavior pleases you very much. It is counterproductive to attempt to alter your dog's behavior. What is useful is to attempt to alter his environment so that his natural behavior coincides with your needs. In the matter of housebreaking, it is simply a question of extending the animal's territory to the outdoors so that he may stake his claim there instead of on your carpet.

"Dogs do not behave out of spite or guilt. Most problem behavior stems from fear or boredom." *Gaines*

How to Housebreak Your Dog

(1) Select a place outdoors as the toilet ground. Use this locale consistently. (2) Until the dog is housebroken, confine his movements in the house to one room. If he is allowed out of the restricted area, watch him at all times. (3) Take the dog to the toilet area first thing in the morning and last thing in the evening, after each meal, after drinking water, after a nap, after a vigorous play or exercise period. (4) Praise the dog immediately after he relieves himself, outdoors and at the toilet area. (5) Bring him indoors immediately after toileting. Do not let him misinterpret the outing as a play period. (6) Take your dog outside when he gives signals for eliminating such as sniffing the ground or turning in circles. (7) Feed your dog on a consistent schedule so that his need to eliminate will also be on a consistent schedule. If you plan to put him on a self-feeding program, do not start it until he is housebroken. (8) Do not punish the dog if he has an accident. If you catch him in the act, say "No!" in a harsh voice and rush him outdoors to his toilet location. P.S.: Keep a bottle of Nilotex around for urine stains and Airwick's Carpet Fresh as a rug and room deodorizer.

Using A Dog Crate For Housebreaking

A dog crate is a wire rectangle with a metal or wood floor and can be purchased in a size suitable for each dog. It only *looks* like a cage with a door. If used properly it ties in directly with your dog's instincts to have a den as the core area of his territory. A dog crate is a sanctuary for your pet. *From the dog's view it is not so much that he cannot get out but rather that you cannot get in.* However, the crate is much more than a sanctuary. It is an extremely useful tool when housebreaking your dog—whether he be a puppy, adolescent or adult animal.

Housebreaking a puppy begins the day he comes into your home. It can take as little as three days and as long as three weeks. During the period of housebreaking the pup should not have the run of the house without being carefully watched. Crate the dog at all other times. His inclination not to soil his den will work for you.

Place the puppy on a strict FEED-WATER-WALK-CRATE schedule. Adhere to the established schedule consistently so as to regulate the dog's digestive system.

From the dog's view it is not so much that he cannot
get out but rather that you cannot get in. *Tom O'Shea*

Early morning	Walk the dog and return to crate
One half hour later	Feed, water, walk and return to crate
Mid-morning	Water, walk and return to crate
Past noon	Feed, water, walk and return to crate
Mid-afternoon	Water, walk and return to crate
Late afternoon	Water, walk and return to crate
Early evening	Feed, water, walk and return to crate
Before retiring	Walk the dog and return to crate for the night

During the day and evening you may remove the puppy from the crate any time for play and attention. Watch for sniffing and circling as signs for the dog's need to go outside. Do not feed or water the dog at night during the housebreaking period. Do not give the puppy any food or treats between scheduled meals. Stick closely to the schedule. Do not punish the dog for mistakes. Correct him by saying "NO" in a firm voice and remove him to the outdoors to finish. Always praise the puppy for doing the right thing. In a short time the dog will go to the door or give you some other signal to be let out. When that happens, his housebreaking training is complete.

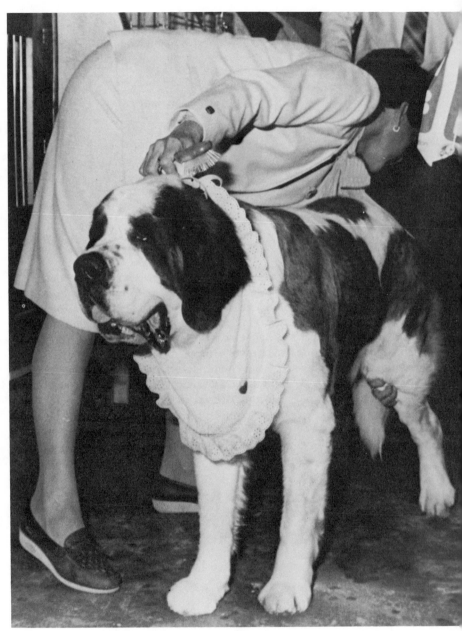

4

The Health Club

A PAUNCHY POOCH with sagging shoulders and dragging tail can be a victim of urban blight like any other dweller in the cities of America. The stresses and strains of modern living have their bad effect on dogs as they do on humans. Overcrowding, violence, the exigencies of economic strain, noise, dirt, and supersonic change cause headaches, nervous breakdowns, and death at the higher end of the scale, and listlessness, overweight, and physical deterioration at the lower end. Modern dogs, like modern humans, must take better care of themselves or suffer the consequences. Of course, dogs need more help than humans in this respect. You'll never get a dog to count calories or meditate on his own. And you can forget the daily regimen of the Royal Canadian Air Force Exercises. Dogs are just not self-starters. Those living the good life, all fat and sassy, never think about that great resort in the sky where existence is less than a TV dog-food commercial. Dogs of America! Shape up! Dogs and their owners must learn to relax, to eat sensibly and to get out there and do some exercise.

A young woman fell from her high perch into the ravine and

sank down into the fast-rushing stream of water. The large Saint Bernard heard her cry for help while lying on its side, still dazed from being clubbed on the head by the dope smuggler in the checkered shirt. The noble dog somehow staggered to his feet and made a start for the edge of the cliff. He was confronted by a mean-looking Rottweiler. The villainous dog snarled, but the Saint Bernard growled such a menacing sound from deep within the throat that the black and tan Rottweiler backed away, turned and ran. With that chore settled, he cautiously went to the edge and looked down from the height. He could see his mistress trying to stay above the water as she flailed about. With the determined look of a hero, the dog stood at the edge and poised for the long plunge downward.

"Cut. That's a take," yelled the director. "Set up for shot 215, the dive. Get the stunt dog in makeup."

Mortimer was probably the most beautiful Saint Bernard in the country; at least his millions of fans thought so. The large, noble dog was a film and TV star of great magnitude. He was more than a film star. He was an industry unto himself with Mortimer T-shirts, bubble-gum cards, wristwatches, and board games. The great dog was seen on billboards across the nation and on countless TV commercials selling everything from mutual funds to feminine sprays. The most popular breakfast cereal ran continuing stories of his exploits on the back of the boxes, and charities and businesses competed fiercely for his endorsement.

Mortimer's coat was dazzling in its orange-red and white colors, with black fur around the eyes and ear tops which hung down like velvet flaps. His tail was a brilliant splash of red and white that made his fans scream whenever he waved it in their faces. The Saint Bernard was the star attraction wherever he went. He was seven years old, but the studio publicists claimed he was five. They also planted items in the papers about Mortimer's being something of a ladies' dog, what with a fling with a lovely Afghan here and a Borzoi there. The truth of the matter is that the handsome brute suffered from cryptorchidism (a congenital condition in which the testicles have not descended; such dogs are usually sterile) and could never qualify for an American Kennel Club show competition. Uneasy lies the head that wears a crown.

Because Mortimer's fame was so great, his worth to his owner and movie studio was in the millions of dollars. Consequently, they never took chances with his well-being. Despite the fact that his fame was based on heroic exploits, they never allowed him to actually perform the daring deeds. Contagion Filmway Studios had insured him for $15,000,000, and the policy stipulated that all actions involving potentially hazardous consequences to life and limb had to be performed by other dogs. So the studio purchased a stable of Saint Bernard stunt dogs who, though valuable themselves, never came close to the star's value.

Mortimer began life in an exclusive kennel with parents who were AKC Champions of Record. Because of the puppy's splendid conformation, it was assumed that he would make a great show dog. As he got a little older it became apparent that he suffered from cryptorchidism and that would keep him out of the show ring for the rest of his life. As a matter of fact, the kennel owners were seriously considering destroying him. If it weren't for George Atkins, the local mailman, Mortimer would never have seen his fifth month.

George wanted a large dog to walk his mail route with him for company and for protection from other dogs that always attacked him. For two years George and Mortimer delivered mail together and had a great time. One day a film crew showed up in the small town to shoot a commercial. The director of the unit decided he wanted a dog in the background after he spotted Mortimer and George Atkins walking their mail route. The owners of the product being advertised in the commercial liked Mortimer's looks and personality and asked for a commercial using the dog as the main character. The rest is show-business history. From TV commercials to a TV series to a string of successful motion pictures was the story of "Mortimer— Everybody's Dog."

George Atkins had the good sense not to accept the $5,000 offered to him by the original director. And so, Mortimer and George lived in Beverly Hills in a house with a swimming pool, protected from the public by iron gates, private guards, and patrol dogs. Of course, George gave up his mail route, but the Postal Service gave him a special status so that he would not lose his pension. After all, you never know. In exchange, George gave the Postal Service the right to use Mortimer's image as "The Postman's Friend," a poster hanging on post-office walls everywhere.

George loved Mortimer as he did in the past, when they simply delivered mail together; but as the dog became an important star, George began relating to the dog from an attitude of inferiority. The relationship really started to deteriorate when George began

63

knocking on the door before entering a room where Mortimer was lying around. Of course, the studio representative's snide attitude toward George was an important inhibiting factor in the relationship. The studio man was intolerant and distant with George and made him feel in the way. The former mailman was constantly excusing himself (even to the dog) as he indulged the animal's every whim. All the dog seemed to want, however, was to see more of George, who was trying to stay out of his way.

Mortimer was now a movie star, and like many people, George was intimidated by this—so intimidated that he lost sight of the fact that Mortimer was a dog and he was a human being. "Pack" status was now all twisted around. George had given up his leadership position, which might have been fine if they were both wolves living in the wild.

Little by little, the representatives of the studio took over the care and maintenance of the dog star. With bruised feelings of inferiority, George retreated to his part of the house and appeared only now and again to sign contracts. He missed the dog terribly and the dog missed him, but he was too depressed to understand what was happening. He no longer supervised Mortimer's diet. No longer took him for walks. No longer spent those harrowing hours giving the big fellow baths and brushings. George felt it was better that the studio pros do those things. After all, Mortimer was now an important public figure, and what would he want with a common mailman? It was the warm, loving contact of those daily brushings that Mortimer missed most of all. He did not understand why his master rarely touched him anymore.

With George no longer an obstacle, the studio publicity department started scheduling one public appearance after another. The dog's appearances were now booked five and six days at a time. They'd fly him in a private jet across the country to ride in an open-top limousine as the grand marshal of some parade and then fly him to another city for the opening ceremonies of a humane shelter. The dog was pushed and shoved and carted and petted and oohed and aahed with no regular eating schedule and certainly no time for himself.

On the set, it was the same. Just as the script was getting good and Mortimer was supposed to do something interesting, the director would yell "Cut" and call for the stunt dogs. Poor Mortimer was starting to feel as useful as Trigger, stuffed and mounted in Roy Rogers' backyard.

All communication between Mortimer and George ceased, and this had a profound emotional effect on the large dog. When a dog lives with one human for five years and has been subordinate to that person, it is no easy adjustment to accept a reversal of roles and finally a rupture in the relationship. Mortimer missed the loving hands that fed, walked, bathed, brushed, and disciplined him. He was a dog, and he missed his master. He hadn't the slightest idea that humans had transformed him into a film deity. Whenever he saw himself on the screen, he thought he was looking at another dog. When confronted with a crowd of fans, he searched for the one face that he wanted to see the most. He was constantly disappointed and it began to take its toll. The large Saint Bernard was beginning to feel the physical consequences of emotional stress and lack of proper care.

It was about this time that the trouble began. Mortimer was being groomed for a scene that he was to shoot in one hour. To the groomer's horror he found two bald patches about the size of a dime on Mortimer's forehead. At the same time, one of the handlers told the director that the dog had not touched his food all day and that the star was lethargic and disinterested in everything.

A veterinarian was summoned immediately and, to the embarrassment of everyone on the set, a rectal temperature reading was taken. The crew immediately set up some screens to give the dog privacy. The vet told the studio head, who had by this time dropped everything and come down to the set, that Mortimer had demodectic mange, caused by tiny mites that burrow tunnels into the skin and cause the loss of fur, underneath which was red, scaly skin. The vet said that it was not serious for the moment, but that Mortimer would have to have much of his coat shaved off so that other infected parts of the body could be seen and treated. The doctor was indignant and spoke harshly. The dog was run down, and that was probably the main cause of the disease. It was pointed out that Mortimer had put on too much weight, did not seem to be getting a balanced diet and that his muscle tone was atrocious.

"How much exercise does this animal get?" asked the vet. No one answered.

"No one knows," muttered the doctor. "Okay, how many walks in a day does he get?" There was no answer. In truth, no one knew because no one exercised the dog. He was allowed to relieve himself anywhere he wanted to, so he didn't even get walked for that purpose.

"This dog is a physical wreck. Who's responsible for his welfare?" asked Dr. Bolton looking into the crowd of studio representatives.

"George Atkins, I guess," answered one of the executives.

"Well," said the vet, "you get him over and take this dog home. He's gonna need a new set of ears when I get through with him. I'll tell you, I'll get a court order and have the SPCA come get this animal unless he isn't taken better care of."

"Where the hell is George Atkins?" shouted the studio head. "Send a car for him. You tell us what to do, doc, and it'll be done."

In a cowed and conciliatory manner, the head of the studio pleaded with George Atkins to step back into the picture and take care of his dog once again. At first the old letter carrier was reluctant to get involved.

"Mortimer is an important dog, and I wouldn't want to interfere with his life. There's no dignity being supported by a dog, you know."

The studio head was irritated. He replied. "You damn fool. That dog needs you. Don't you see what's happening to him? For God's sake, he's falling apart!"

George wiped his eyes and blew his nose and gave the matter serious consideration. His reply was given slowly and with much emotion.

"I love that old boy and wouldn't want any harm to come to him. I guess I'll just let him know that. Where is he now?"

Within minutes the old "pack" was reunited and put on the old footing. Both George and Mortimer immediately began to feel better.

With a lot of care and attention, Mortimer's mange began to heal. Twice a week the Saint Bernard was given a mineral oil bath and then dabbed with a liquid medication. Of course he looked awful with half his long coat shaved off. He resembled a barber's pole with a face. The handsome movie star was the worst he had ever looked in his life.

A sensible nutritional regimen was established: a good balance of high-quality protein, fat carbohydrates, vitamins, and minerals. Catered buffets and exotic people-food were removed from the dog's diet. In addition, George saw to it that the dog was exercised every day. But probably the most important aspect of Mortimer's cure was the reestablishment of his relationship with George Atkins. His owner suffered much guilt about the dog's poor health and worked very hard to make up for lost time. He wasn't about to let Mortimer down again.

George's answer to the problem was to get himself reinstated with the Postal Service. He was given a short mail route in the exclusive community of Beverly Hills. The reason for taking another mail route was for Mortimer's sake. Every morning and every afternoon, plain old George the Mailman hiked up and down the manicured Hills of Beverly followed by his mangy-looking dog, Mortimer. Many a movie star was handed his mail by an equally famous colleague without knowing who it was. No one suspected. Not even the head of Contagion Filmway Studios, who lived down the road. Mortimer's film was held up in production while his fellow actors (and stunt dogs) waited for his long coat to grow back to normal. But somehow it was quite clear that things were going to be different. In the meantime, the mail must go through.

Mortimer was not fed properly, nor did he receive the exercise so important for a dog his size. He was driven to a state of nervous exhaustion by living in an atmosphere of great pressure and tension. Couple that with a lack of affection, and you have the perfect conditions for physical and emotional breakdown. This much stress can cause a great deal more than just demodectic mange. Lack of exercise, poor diet, excess weight, long work hours, disruption of the normal routine, and lack of emotional contact can lead to heart disease, dermatitis, arthritis, allergies, chronic diarrhea, ulcers, viral infections, disorders of the nervous system, and dozens of other ailments and diseases.

It has been reported that wolves spend one-third of their day traveling, one-third stalking prey, and one-third sleeping. Between summer and winter they may travel as much as 500 miles to keep up with the herd prey. This may explain why wolves, cousins of domestic dogs, are always in lean, hard shape. Only those that go hungry are in as bad shape as many pet dogs. The reason is diet and physical activity.

The wolf travels great distances and works quite hard for his living in the course of one day. This may give us a general idea of the physical activity required by domestic dogs to keep them healthy. There are many factors to consider when determining what the exercise requirements are of individual dogs. Size is certainly an important factor. The larger the body, the more movement it will take to keep the muscles (including the heart) in tone. Weight and daily activity also play a part in one's exercise choices. Weather and climatic conditions are equally important. One of the best ways to determine how much exercise to give a dog is to investigate what employment his breed was developed for. The Saint Bernard, for example, was developed for its strength so that it could successfully work as a rescue dog in the Alps. Its powerful build and acute sense of smell allowed it to rescue thousands of people in past centuries trapped beneath fallen snow in the St. Bernard Pass in Switzerland.

A small lapdog, living indoors in a temperate climate, is certainly not going to require the same amount of exercise as an outdoor sporting dog such as a Pointer or an Irish Setter. Overweight middle-aged dogs should be exercised more than trim adolescent ones. It's all a matter of common sense.

Although by necessity your dog's exercise is dictated by the time available for it to be given, some aspects of physical activity must be understood. The dog began as an outdoor creature, carving out territory, fighting to keep it, hunting great distances for food, migrating when the food stock migrated, and protecting its young. The domestic version of the wild dog remains possessed by many of the same instincts and resulting physical and emotional needs. All dogs have the instinct to hunt (with or without the talent for it) and build up a great deal of energy that must be released. Like caged animals in the zoo, they must be let out of their apartments and houses and given a workout. It's not only important physically, but emotionally as well.

When considering your dog's exercise, do not be fooled by size. Although most toy breeds require minimal amounts of exercise, some of the small terriers need more than their size would seem to indicate. The smallest of terriers were hunters at one time, and they still have a lot of steam to work off. The working breeds, the hounds, the sporting breeds, many of the terriers (certainly the larger ones), and

One of the finest exercises for a dog is playing fetch with a Frisbee flying disc. Pictured is Ashley Whippet working out with the author. *Cycle*

various nonsporting breeds such as Dalmatians, Poodles, and Schipperkes all need from moderate to vigorous workouts. Remember, working dogs used to labor from eight to fourteen hours a day. Sporting dogs may have run through fields and bush for as far as 20 miles in one morning. All dogs need exercise.

Most family dogs never get more exercise than a twice-a-day walk. Except for the trip from fireplug to fridge, Phydeaux mostly lies in the corner with one eye on the can opener and the other on Monday Night Football.

Exercise, however, is not only important for your dog's body for his mental stability as well. Inactivity will certainly get your dog out of good physical shape quickly, and that can mean more trips to the vet than normal. Moreover, lethargy will bring on boredom and, perhaps, anxiety, which are the foundations for most forms of antisocial behavior such as chewing, howling, barking and biting.

The best exercise for puppies of any breed is free play with another dog or several toys and a human. (They stop when tired.) Giving your adult dog a long, hard run once a day or several times a week is wonderful. Though most country dogs have no difficulty getting this, there are ways city dogs can run off their pent-up frustrations too.

One way is to jog along with a master or mistress—but this must be done with intelligence. To joggers eager to share the sport with their pets, here is some advice: *Have your pet checked by a vet. Condition your pet for distance, speed, weather conditions and jogging surfaces through a planned, progressive program. Start off slowly. Watch the dog for signs of fatigue and discomfort. At the first indication of discomfort, stop and rest. Keep your jogging pet on a leash. A dog is safer jogging in the morning or at night than during the day when the temperature and humidity are the highest.* The most serious effect of pushing dogs beyond their physical limits is heat prostration, so keep this in mind and jog with caution.

Other forms of canine exercise include basic obedience courses and practice; swimming; field trials; obedience trials; dog shows; homemade obstacle courses; and playing fetch with a Frisbee flying disk. Few dogs can resist the throw and fetch of this absolutely super exercise. Outdoors, in parks and backyards, the disk sails through the air, offering your dog a running/retrieving game that must have been invented in doggy heaven. Indoors, the disk must be tossed in a gentler manner so that it doesn't go through a pane of glass.

Even city dogs can jog along with their owners. Be sure to have your pet checked out by a veterinarian before beginning any vigorous exercise regimen. *M. Siegal*

New York dog trainer Nancy Strauss has an exercise she calls *puppy push-ups:* Give your obedience-trained dog the command *sit* followed by the command *down* 10 or 15 times. It will provide a decent workout.

Exercising your best friend is fun, healthy and humane. Get your dog out of the sack and into the physical fitness bag—he'll love you for it.

Do not exercise an older dog too strenuously. An animal recovering from illness must be allowed to rest and regain strength. Some large to oversized breeds are predisposed to a very serious ailment known as "bloat." It is rare but very serious and can lead to death. Bloat comes after eating and is sometimes connected with strenuous exercise. The stomach may twist in such a way that it prevents expanding gas from leaving the body, and the dog literally swells up like a basketball. It is very painful. If you own a dog as large as a Great Dane or Saint Bernard, it is best to avoid gaseous vegetables such as cauliflower or broccoli. Do not allow your dog to exercise strenuously before or after meals. If symptoms of bloat appear, see a veterinarian immediately.

Some dogs frequent the vet's office on a revolving door basis with far too many ailments while others go once a year for a checkup. Nothing stresses a dog more than sickness and the ensuing therapy. Chronic illness takes its emotional toll.

Although there are no pat answers that apply to all dogs in terms of preventive medicine, there are some general guidelines that have a good effect. The areas of prevention sort themselves into several categories. These represent the foundation for good, basic dog care and should, in most cases, keep the typical house dog in fine fettle.

Vaccinations

The average adult dog should be inoculated for distemper, infectious hepatitis, parainfluenza (the two or three types of kennel coughs for which your vet is vaccinating), parvovirus, leptospirosis, and rabies. Vaccination types and schedules vary from doctor to doctor. In addition to varying points of view, different regions of the country are affected by statute and local conditions.

Unfortunately, some pet owners incorrectly believe a dog's basic shots are permanent, but most vaccinations require annual booster shots. Some vaccines are good for one, two or even three years. Ask your veterinarian.

Nutrition

For most dogs the best food is a premium commercial preparation that states on its label "100% complete" or "complete and balanced diet." These labels mean the food contains the correct proportions of protein, fat, carbohydrates, vitamins and minerals that have been established by the National Academy of Science. These commercial preparations can be canned meat and meat by-products, soft-moist food or dry cereal types. Dry cereal-type food averages between 1,600 and 1,700 calories per pound; regular canned mixtures contain approximately 500 calories per can and soft-moist products average between 1,400 and 1,500 calories per pound. The typical adult dog who is an outdoor house pet requires approximately 30 to 40 calories per pound of body weight each day. Active dogs require at least 40 to 50 calories per pound of body weight each day. For more information write to Pet Food Institute, Suite 1150, 1730 Pennsylvania Ave., NW, Washington, DC 20006.

Grooming

Grooming is essential for good canine hygiene. All dogs, long- and short-coated, should be brushed daily to remove dead hair and dandruff. Long-haired dogs will develop mats, tangles and knots if they are not frequently brushed and combed. This not only cleans the coat and stimulates the skin, but also helps control dermatological ailments. Daily or even weekly grooming sessions allow the pet owner to catch significant body abnormalities such as lumps, lesions, cuts, scratches and even external parasites in their beginning stages. Nothing is more useful than frequent home examinations. Other important aspects of grooming and hygiene are baths, nail clipping, eye and ear cleaning, and the investigation of obvious body odors.

Internal Parasites

Internal parasites (worms and one-celled animals) are common among dogs and must be treated quickly. The most common are roundworms, whipworms, hookworms, tapeworms and heartworms. Depending upon the degree of infestation, the condition may be mildly harmful or gravely serious; if caught, its treatment in most cases is simple and 100-percent effective.

As the parasites are often detectable only with a microscope, samples of your dog's stool should be laboratory-tested by a veterinarian two or three times a year. Heartworm tests require blood samples. Once a dog is tested and found to be free of heartworms, a preventive medication may be prescribed by the vet.

Most internal parasites are transmitted through fecal contact. Always walk your dog on-leash and prevent him/her from coming in contact with other dog's feces. Tapeworms are transmitted through intermediate hosts such as fleas, vermin or infested raw meat. Monthly wormers are not recommended because they are ineffective against all parasites and amount to a gratuitous ingestion of drugs.

External Parasites

Fleas, ticks, lice and mites are the primary villains that latch on to the outer body of the dog. The part of the country one lives in determines whether the problem is seasonal or year-round. In areas with warm or humid weather, such as Florida or California, fleas and ticks will be seen all the time. The local veterinarian is the best person to ask about this problem.

Once a dog becomes infested with an external parasite, his body must be treated with some form of pesticide. Sprays, dips, soaps and shampoos are all effective except in the case of mites. These microscopic parasites must be diagnosed and treated by a veterinarian. All areas that the dog inhabits must then be cleaned thoroughly with soap and water and attacked with a proper pesticide. A professional exterminator may be needed because it is absolutely essential to kill the insects in and around the house plus the eggs that may hatch several days after a clean out.

Dental Care

Much dental work performed by veterinarians would be

unnecessary if proper care were taken by the owner. Tartar accumulates constantly in a dog's mouth and should be removed on a regular basis to prevent mouth odor, gum disease and loss of teeth. Brush the animal's teeth once a week with a soft toothbrush or cotton swab dipped in a paste of warm water and table salt or baking soda. This will save you costly vet bills and avoid the use of anesthesia, which is dangerous for older dogs especially, when removing tartar buildup.

Emotional Environment

Emotional stress can shorten a dog's life as surely as any disease. Anxiety can bring about various forms of physical stress. However, it is not difficult to maintain a dog in an anxiety-free condition.

Routines, habits and established behavior patterns should be respected and maintained where possible. Touch your dog when expressing affection and talk to him, too. Try not to separate him from his home or family. Do not holler at him. Do not hit him.

Medical Care

Have the dog examined by a veterinarian at least once a year, more if the dog is ill or older. Watch for signs of illness and do not wait before seeing the doctor—early treatment sometimes avoids life-threatening disease. When the dog is not acting like himself call your vet and ask for advice.

Keeping a dog in a keen state of mental and physical health is a matter of great concern to most dog owners. Certainly the family veterinarian assumes much of the responsibility for the latter (providing the dog owner heeds the doctor's advice), but the former really lies at the feet of each individual owner.

5

Training Dogs

You're walking your dog on a nice, sunny day. A friend greets you and all three of you stop. You say, "Wolfgang, sit." Your dog makes a slight gesture at sitting. He has never been taught the command "sit" and has never been taught the meaning of the word.

A similar system is used by Professor Harold Hill in *The Music Man.* He called it the Think System of teaching music. The only problem with it is that dogs cannot receive mental telepathic messages—at least not in verbal terms.

You start to chew the fat with your friend and become involved in some tidbit of gossip. Wolfgang smells a dried urine spot on the curb, stretches the leash to its fullest, and jerks for the invisible deliciousness. You pull him back in the middle of who's doing it to whom and in a very annoyed tone whine, "Sit." A cute cocker spaniel waddles by flapping her ears and tail in the middle of who died and of what cause. Wolfgang goes crackers and bolts for the tantalizing young thing. You jerk him so hard that all fours leave the ground as you shout, "SIT, DAMN IT, SIT!" Wolfgang leaves you alone as you continue your conversation. The talk ends, you say good-bye, and depart. As you step away, you realize that Wolfgang has dumped on your shoe, and suddenly you understand why the Edwardians wore spats and high-button shoes. As the man once said, "What we have here is a failure to communicate."

Make no mistake about it, dog training involves manipulative techniques for altering your dog's behavior patterns. It all depends on how it's done as to whether it has any negative or personality-change effects on both you and the dog. In human terms we run great risks in a personal relationship when we try to manipulate another human being. In training dogs, there is really no other choice because of the animal's limited abilities to understand what you want and expect and, of course, because dogs do not have a language capacity. Manipulation of dog behavior runs quite a gamut from begging on your knees to dastardly physical abuse. A dog that is thrashed soundly may eventually do what is expected, but at a tremendous cost to his dignity, his rights as one of God's creatures, and his delightful potential as a friend and companion. A dog that is thrashed regularly will eventually become dangerous to himself and to the psychoneurotic coward that beats him. In a last stand at dignity, a battered dog will fight back and get a few slashes and tears in before he is disposed of.

Of course, the most common negative training situation is when the dog is treated like a divinity and asked to suffer the poor humans who come as supplicants, begging for his cooperation. Forget it! A young dog's mind has to be played like a harp to make it work for his master. It requires subtlety, consistency, and a sure-footed knowledge of what you are doing.

———————

Wendel McCoy was a professor of English literature at Chapel Hill University in North Carolina. He was one of those rare men who could heat rolls by talking to them. His students adored him because he was able to communicate to them what he had in mind, and what he had in mind was usually to their liking. One of his newer and more original teaching themes was "Writers and Their Pets." It was different and quite captivating to study the relationships between T.S. Eliot and his cats as revealed in his *Old Possum's Book of Practical Cats* or Eugene O'Neill's *The Last Will and Testament of an Extremely Distinguished Dog*. Paul Gallico, Ogden Nash, James

Thurber, Dickens, Kipling, Twain, Faulkner, Terhune all lived out their canine and feline literary creations and had special feelings about them. Virginia Woolf wrote a biography of Flush, the much-adored Cocker Spaniel owned by Elizabeth Barrett Browning. Mackinlay Kantor's *Lobo* and Jack London's masterpiece, *The Call of the Wild,* were all part of the course which was described by all McCoy's students as "wonderful." At the end of the year, they bought him an English Springer Spaniel puppy because they felt it best suited his personal glow and tweedy self. The day they presented the little critter, it was *Goodbye, Mr. Chips* all the way. McCoy was very touched by the gesture, which he secretly expected. It also scared the hell out of him. He didn't really like dogs and knew very little about them and their ways.

He knew enough to spread out newspapers on the kitchen floor and confine the little guy there at night. But for many weeks he did little more than that. Somehow the dog, now named *Kant,* couldn't. He couldn't stop from chewing the baseboards. He couldn't exercise enough self-control to avoid lifting his hind leg and watering the housekeeper's tulip bulbs. He couldn't do one single thing that was asked of him.

The first time McCoy took him out, he tied a stylish red bandanna around the dog's neck instead of a sturdy leather collar. Then the good professor tied an eight-foot piece of manila hemp around the bandanna to serve as one of the longest puppy leashes in recorded history. All the dog needed was a sombrero and a gold tooth and he could have been cast in a remake of *The Treasure of the Sierra Madre.* It was particularly busy on the town streets, with a great deal of car and truck traffic. McCoy carried the puppy to the sidewalk and set him down with great expectations of taking a casual constitutional . . . just a man and his dog.

As the dog touched the sidewalk, a rattling pickup truck in dire need of a new muffler quaked its way up the street. The little dog ran the full eight feet of the yellow rope and cringed in terror against the nearest wall. McCoy was almost dragged off his feet. He pulled at the rope, gently at first, trying to get the dog to walk. Kant shivered as he tried to integrate into the wall. With determined force McCoy yanked the leash, but still the dog wouldn't budge. Finally, with all his might, he jerked the rope and socked his own jaw with both his fists, which were tightly clutched. For an instant the scholarly dog owner saw stars and heard bells. Having recovered, he carried the dog home

Here is the English Springer Spaniel doing what it has been bred to do. Its accomplishments are due in part to good breeding and in part to good training. Dogs cannot be trained without being conditioned by specific training techniques. One can engage the services of a professional trainer, attend a dog training class, or do it at home with the help of a dog training book. *Tom O'Shea*

79

noticing that his paws had been scraped against the sidewalk so hard that there was a little blood showing through the pads.

The next step in the little dog's education was to teach his master that he didn't want to come to him every time he was called. "C'mon, Kant, let's go, boy. Here. Come here, will you please? Mr. McCoy's got a biscuit for you." Success. All McCoy had to do was pull out a dog biscuit and the dog would appear at his feet with all the loyalty of a nineteenth-century camel driver. The small Springer had a real craving for the cookielike biscuits and was a sucker for a bribe. However, if the good professor was not prepared with payola when he called the dog, nothing happened. The young extortionist would barely turn away from his current activity, which could be anything from eating the couch to claiming a far wall with his hind leg raised. The unflappable Wendel McCoy would quietly walk away from the indifferent dog like an experimenter going back to the drawing board. The principal difference was that he never had a new or better idea how to communicate with the animal. It never occurred to him that he should be the dominant figure in their relationship. He conducted his pet stewardship in strictly egalitarian terms. He thought it was the democratic thing to do. What actually existed was a dog dictatorship with he, the human, brought to his knees with a paw on his neck. It was not so much a humiliation as it was a boring waste of time.

Finally, McCoy's three-times-a-week housekeeper, Mrs. Gladys Coldstream, had a showdown.

"Dr. McCoy," she started out as she braced herself against the edge of the sink, "something's got to change here."

"What are you talking about?"

"That little beast with the liver-flap ears, that's what I'm talking about. So far he's eaten my electric orange juicer, half of my mixer, an entire spatula, and the hose off your Water-Pic. And that's not to mention the crappola neatly positioned at the base of my tulip stems. You don't have a sock left without a hole in the toe, and he's twice stepped into biscuit batter." The old gray workhorse with her solid square jaw began to cry.

"If you don't do something about that rotten dog, (she shouts) I WILL!"

"What can you do? What would you do?"

"Oh," she said, shaking her head and her fist, "I'd give him a dog lesson. Don't you see, he's got to be made to understand about dogs and people."

80

"How'd you like to explain that to me?" said McCoy.

"It's really very simple. The first time he gets out of line, you step on his neck and holler like hell. Eventually he'll get the idea."

McCoy rubbed his chin, hoping an answer would come out of his mouth like a penny fortune. He didn't like the sound of what Coldstream had in mind.

"I think you'd better let me handle it."

"Sure," she yelled, "you handle it—or I will. Remember, my foot three feet up you-know-what."

Later that evening, after a cold dinner, McCoy decided that if he could tame cages full of undergraduates, there was no reason why he couldn't get through to a simple-minded *Canis familiaris.* "Say what you have in mind in the most honest and sincere fashion, with firmness and reason," he thought. "Sure, have a talk with the poor fellow. No wonder he doesn't do anything right. We don't understand each other. Most assuredly he'll apply himself to the problem at hand once I explain that he's not working up to his full potential. Yes, that's it. We'll have a talk. And when it's over, he'll understand that my success is determined by how well he does around here. It's on him."

Feeling an expansive glow, McCoy left his coffee cup on the arm of his stuffed chair and went looking for Kant.

"Hey, boy. Yo, Kant. Where are you, kiddo?"

Kant did not answer.

With glasses in hand, he searched throughout the small cottage but could not find one trace of the adolescent Springer. Deciding to warm up to the heart-to-heart before they sat down, McCoy yelled out, "Oh, Kant. Did you know that the word *spaniel* literally means a Spanish dog. And *springer* derives from Old English *spring,* itself from Old English *springan,* to leap, whence, via Middle English *springen,* and finally to the English 'to spring,' occasionally used as *sprung.* That must mean you are an Hispanic canine with a predisposition toward jumping on things. Logic, my friend. That's what makes the world turn 'round. Logic."

With that the horn-rimmed logician entered the inner sanctum of his bedroom. There he found Kant sitting next to his chest of drawers. It dated back to 1609. The elaborate chest was hand carved, painted and ornamented with Elizabethan strapwork inlaid into the brightly painted wood. It was an especially rare and expensive piece of furniture.

McCoy began rubbing his hand when he saw the results of Kant's preoccupation. Half the patina was licked away from the third drawer from the top. The lower two drawers had the painted wood surfaces chewed off the base material to reveal that it was only a veneer covering hardwood underneath. The mutilated chest was a fake and not worth fussing over what the dog had done to it. McCoy felt as though a bell clapper struck him first on one side of his head and then the other. He did not pass out as he should have. He tore at the bulging vein in his neck and shrieked out something that sounded like "Spanish swine." With two arms extended like a frothing madman wanting to strangle, he chased the dog around the house. There was smashing and kicking and yelling and puppy howling and finally low-throated sobbing. Their talk was over. The next day Wendel McCoy went on a two-year sabbatical and Kant went to live with Mrs. Coldstream. She was determined to teach him about dogs and people and tulip stems.

———————

Training a dog can be an emotional business if you are not working from sound principles and techniques. There are three training facts that the good professor McCoy did not understand about dog training. One: a dog is genetically organized to live and function within the demands of a pack structure based on dominance and subordination. Two: the ideal time to create within the animal a susceptibility to obedience training is precise and predetermined. And three: there is a teaching process which is based on the Pavlovian principles of conditioned reflexes reinforced with rewards and punishments (replace the word punishments with corrections).

Dogs do not have the mental capacities of human beings, obviously, and therefore nothing Wendel McCoy could have said to his dog would have made the slightest difference in dog training. To merely tell a dog to sit on command means nothing. He must be *taught* how to sit and made to associate the utterance of the word with the action of sitting. The action must then be reinforced with a pleasant reward, thus conditioning him to do as you command out of an uncontrollable desire to obey. If it sounds like mind bending, that's exactly what it is. It is also referred to as behavior modification.

One need only study the social structure of the wolf pack to understand the most basic life-style of the domestic dog. Sometimes wolf packs are comprised of blood relations and sometimes combinations of relatives and close neighbors of circumstance. Hunting, mating, and carving out territory, the essentials for survival in the wild, are accomplished as a group effort. However, there is a chain of command involving a leader of the pack and the various lesser lights of the pecking order. The leader is determined by size and the pugnaciously won right to lead. Once the lead wolf is determined, the lower-ranking wolves sort themselves out and find themselves relegated to various tasks and privileges based on rank.

This life-style is basic from the first waking moments of a domestic dog's life. Entering into a human/canine situation does not alter the dog's instincts. He merely transfers the instinct for social structure to the human condition and transposes the idea of "pack" into the more familiar condition known as "family." Now, his instinct is to either lead the family (pack) or be led by the strongest member(s). From the dog's point of view, a leader is absolutely necessary, and he will take the job if only by default of the human members of the pack. The dog's instinct for survival forces him to fill the position of leader if no member of the family takes the responsibility. Therefore, in order to train a dog, he must be relegated to the status of subordinate family member rather than dominant member—or he will not even attempt to learn or obey.

It is now widely accepted that there are critical phases in the earliest weeks of a puppy's life that help shape his ability to be influenced by various environmental factors. The first three weeks (21 days) of a puppy's life are spent developing his sensory and motor capacities. Between the fourth and thirteenth weeks, the adaptability to social relationships is determined if certain conditions are or are not present in the puppy's immediate sensory environment. Isolation during this period will not permit the animal to develop an adaptability to humans or other dogs.

A dog kept exclusively with other dogs and never introduced to humans during this stage will adapt only to the presence of other dogs *throughout his life!* If the dog is exposed to human contact, both sensory and emotional, during this critical period (4-13 weeks), he will become extremely adaptable to human family life and consequently susceptible to obedience training. This is called "socializing." Based on the research of Dr. John Fuller and Dr. John

Paul Scott, the optimum time to remove a puppy from its litter is at the end of the seventh week of life. Between eight and sixteen weeks the dog is not only entering its prime time for adapting to the idea of human acceptance, it is also ready to have circumstances develop the dominant or subordinate inclination with its pack or family. It is then that obedience training has its best opportunity for effectiveness without disturbing the little dog's emotional stability.

Teaching a dog obedience training is a lengthy and technical process, one which cannot be covered in these limited pages. The underlying principles can be given, however, so that almost any manual can be obtained and utilized with utmost efficiency.

When training a dog, the dominant/subordinate relationship is of primary concern. The human being clearly must take a leadership position, and this is accomplished by understanding that you, the human, are the responsible adult in the situation and that your pet is a totally dependent dog. Your voice must be firm and resonant when giving obedience commands (especially during the training sessions). You must maintain a no-nonsense attitude like a commanding officer dealing with a private in the army. Your dog's willingness to obey your commands may save his life some day in a potentially hazardous traffic situation. An obedience-trained dog is less likely to lose his good home or run away and get himself stolen or ensnared by a dog warden.

Taking the dominant position with a puppy is the easiest thing in the world. Simply make him follow you everywhere. Call him to you in a friendly tone of voice (not too exuberantly). Few puppies can resist this. When he runs up to your legs, turn abound and begin walking away. He should follow. Walk a few steps and bend down and pet him and reward him with praise. Repeat this command many times throughout the day. You will be conditioning the animal to follow you and thus take a secondary position with you. His reward is your praise and approval. In this way you have automatically taken the position of pack leader and circumvented the dog's need or desire to take it himself. Once you have assumed that role, you must always play it.

There is no more important aspect to dog training than the behavior of the human being involved. If one were to engage the services of a professional dog trainer one would observe a dominant personality in action. Some trainers are extremely gentle but nevertheless firm and demanding when relating to the dog. If a dog owner decides to train his or her own dog any decent book on the subject demands that the trainer be authoritative (within reason and without abusiveness) not only during the period of training but whenever giving commands.

Did a dog flunk his training course because he continued to yank his owner down the street? What about the pet who begs, whines and generally gets his way? The fault lies not in our pets, dear humans, but in ourselves. All the obedience training in the world will not make a dog behave if the human family is timid or unassertive with the animal.

Dogs who sniff where they shouldn't or march across snowy clean sheets will continue their dreadful habits if they think that they can get away with it.

The inability to be assertive with pets is usually based on a fear that the animal will no longer love the owner if punished or dealt with firmly. (This same misguided kindness is often seen in parents of misbehaved children.) Complicating matters further is the notion that it is cruel to force a pet to stop doing something.

Dogs will not stop loving their owners when the owners decide to take control of their pets' behavior. In fact, it strengthens your rapport with your pet. Asserting yourself with a pet is not an act of cruelty. It isn't even a violation of your animal's true nature. Don't get caught up in the "Born Free" syndrome where everything you do to and for your pet is taken as a violation of the animal's natural inclinations. That attitude has hurt more animals than helped them. Think of what can happen to unleashed dogs that are allowed to roam the streets and roads all day.

Dogs who poke their noses in the garbage can, jump on you or have other annoying habits must be handled in a special way. They require strong leadership and absolute domination. The basis of assertiveness training for pet owners is the knowledge that the pet's very life depends on humans being dominant and animals being subordinate.

In the wild, dogs or wolves develop a highly structured social hierarchy based on dominance and subordination. The dominant *canid* or leader of the pack makes all decisions about mating, hunting, territory and fighting. The pack leader is always the biggest, strongest and most intelligent, commanding respect from all other members of the pack.

In the dog/human equation, think of the family as the pack and you as the leader. The family dog must be considered subordinate to you. This doesn't require an overbearing or abusive manner. Hollering or hitting the animal isn't the answer. Instead, all your assertive action is internal. If you do not feel like a pack leader, then fake it. Think of it as an acting assignment.

Behave like someone who holds the leash rather than someone clipped to it. Remember that *you* are the provider of food, water, shelter and love, and you must act accordingly. It's not necessary to assume the role of commanding officer of an infantry brigade in order to assert yourself. The firm-but-gentle manner of a concerned parent will achieve the best results.

This will be difficult with some dogs, especially those devilishly clever terriers, Dachshunds and Cocker Spaniels. But never let it be said that you were outsmarted by your dog. The next time your dog attempts to steal food from the table or whines at the door when you are not ready for a walk, be sure to assert yourself. One of the best ways to do this is by exclaiming "NO", in a loud, firm tone of voice.

"NO" is the most authoritative and negative word in the language. It is easy to use this term as a corrective tool by firmly establishing its use for bad behavior only. This is essential. Your reprimanding "NO" should be a firm, vocal sound that comes from the diaphragm. Accomplish this by taking in a deep breath and allowing the stomach to expand with air. Say the word "NO" as you release the air. Eventually you will develop a deeper, more resonant sound which will indicate a no-nonsense attitude toward your dog, and not even a Bullmastiff will doubt you. Once you've established that your "NO" means no, be consistent. Never back down.

When you live with a dog, you must learn to be assertive or accept being ruled by a four-pawed dictator. Assertiveness training means never having to say you're sorry!

(Assuming that you have taken the pack-leader position with your young dog, and given that he is "socialized" at the eighth week of life, you are ready to create a perfectly obedience-trained animal.) Using the command "sit" as an example lesson, you must physically force the dog (in a firm but gentle manner) into the sitting position as you say the word.

Push the dog's posterior with your left hand while holding the dog's head by raising the leash slightly upward. Say "sit" in a firm, commanding voice as you do this. Each time the dog is physically forced into the sitting position, praise him lavishly and tell him how good he is. Repeat this command ten, fifteen, or even twenty times during a ten-minute training session. Once your dog seems to understand what the word "sit" means, he may be commanded without being physically positioned. If he obeys the word without being pushed into it, praise him immediately. If he does not obey your vocal command, correct him with a slight jerk of the leash and say "no" firmly. Your dog should sit after the word "No." If he does, praise him. If he doesn't, begin the teaching process over again.

This is precisely how a conditioned reflex is created. An adaptable puppy or adolescent dog seeks your approval and can be taught obedience training by your giving or withholding of praise and by the implementation of correction or punishment gestures, almost always involving a slight side jerk of the leash. Repetition, consistent pack-leader status, rewards, and corrections comprise the formula for simple obedience training. Although it is unthinkable to condition a human being in such oversimplified, manipulative terms, it is a blessing for the dog living in a human family. Here your dog experiences absolute clarity about what is expected of him so that he may live a happy, untroubled existence. Dogs and humans prefer it that way.

He was a serious dresser. *Ken-L-Ration*

6

Sex (Any Dog Can!)

Your DOG consists of bones, muscles, organs, skin, hair, blood, miscellaneous moisture, an electrical system, and an elaborate chemical composition. Dog behavior is tremendously influenced by this physical life as well as by a genetically organized set of instincts coupled with environmental influences. This miraculous feat of divine engineering involves thousands, maybe millions of various intricate functions of the body, not the least of which is cell reproduction and the body's ability to save its own life from the invasions of sickness. Why then all the fuss about getting your dog fixed up with a sultry Ms. or a big daddy stud? Sex is but one lonely function of the mammalian body. It is true that reproduction seems to be the primary force in all of nature. The reasons for this take us by the hand down pathways of philosophy, religion, and the greater questions of existence. But unless you are involved with procreation in order to further some great idea, your dog's genitalia need never come out of the box, so to speak. This, of course, poses the perennial question of many pet owners:

"Does my dog need to experience sex for his mental and physical well-being?" I'm not going to tell you—not yet, anyway.

On certain nights in July, when the air is warm and the water of the East River is cool, a damp, muggy mist tends to fog the evening streets around Sutton Place. The city lamps glow a bright yellow, and the quiet of the lateness seems to amplify every single footstep and occasional tug that slips through the river night. It is a time for lit cigarettes and the clinking against the sidewalk of the metal clips of dog leashes. Shiny leather shoes and dog paws slowly trot through the night on casual missions of search and release. Here and there an occasional meeting takes place in the shadows, and one can only imagine large sums of money being agreed upon and secret meetings being arranged in muffled conversations. Walking a dog on such nights in such streets is a remote but sensual experience. Simon Brace knew all about this, which is why he made the trip every now and again.

He was a serious dresser who wanted to look right even if he was just walking the dog at night. His denim bell-bottoms cut the air with a sharp crease in them, and his tawny Boxer was slick and groomed to a spit shine. Toro's great black jowls glistened with health, and his white diamond-shaped chest could be seen from half a block away. The dog was held by a two-foot-long thickness of heavily stitched cowhide that could have made a pair of cowboy boots. They were an elegant but rugged team, Simon and Toro. As they took their light constitutional, they both searched for that special something hidden in half-conscious dreams. Simon's search was made with 20-20 mobility while Toro kept his nose to the ground hoping to find his dream rubbed into the cement in thin layers of bouquet.

It was just another empty walk that night until Toro's head left the curbstones for the first time. With pricked ears he gazed through the mist and looked for whatever was attached to the sound of the other metal clip heading for him and his master. The dog's sudden reaction alerted Simon, who also looked ahead as he slowed his pace. Like two aircraft coming out of the clouds, an elegant Cocker Spaniel with ears awash and legs in full strut almost collided with brute Boxer. The two dogs suddenly hopped around each other like friends in a distant land and encircled their tethers, one in leather, the other in silver chain. Simon grabbed a quick glance at the beautiful dog's owner and lost his breath. She was in black crepe and lace with a small diamond hanging from her satin blouse. It was hard to see, but the late-show dog walker didn't need a floodlight to know he was in the presence of a once-a-year find. She was lovely—no, she was grand. Looks, style, a gorgeous dog, and obviously a resident of a good neighborhood. She had everything he dreamed of.

"They're a brilliant sight together, aren't they?" offered the owner of Toro.

Lisa Lorna smiled. "Yes, they are. Cushion is two years old next week. How old is . . ."

"Toro," he said with a deep, cleared throat. "Toro's three. Three and half exactly—and six days."

She smiled again and he almost fainted. They just stood there under a street light, allowing the uninhibited investigations of the two dogs to fill the void as they each searched for something to say. Finally:

"They seem to like each other."

"They certainly do," answered Lisa, "Cushy is never this friendly. It must be love."

Without doing a cartwheel, Simon answered, "Yeah," then laughed with neither grace nor wit.

"Has Toro ever serviced a bitch before?"

Sweat dripped from Simon's palms as he replied hoarsely, "Uh, lots of times. What do you think? Of course he has."

"Good," she answered. "Maybe you'd be interested in allowing me to use him for a stud . . . for Cushion. I think they might make interesting puppies. What's his breed?"

"Boxer."

"Well Cushy is a cocker spaniel. If they had puppies that would make them cock-a-boxers, wouldn't it?"

"I guess."

"So, how do you feel about mating these lovers? I'll give you the pick of the litter."

"I consider it a rare opportunity for Toro and me. This is going to be a good thing for him. A dog in the city shouldn't be allowed to remain celibate for too long. It's bad for the environment. It's a matter of ecology and mental health, you know?"

She nodded affirmatively and said, "Great. Where should we do it?"

He swaggered. "Your place or mine? Ha-ha. A little dog humor."

She rolled her eyes at the humor of the question and replied, "Well, I think it's customary to bring the bitch to the stud's run . . ."

Simon opened his mouth as wide as he ever had in thumping anticipation but could not get his answer out in time. "However," she added, "I've got five rooms, and we'll be able to leave them alone. Unless of course you've got five rooms also?"

Once again the injustice of economics defeated Simon Brace, manager of 53rd Street's Hoof and Antler Male Shop. "No, I don't have five rooms. Listen, let's make it at your place. I mean, what's the difference? It's Cushion and Toro's gig, right?"

Four weeks passed, and the delicate Cushion went into heat on schedule. Calls were made and signals sent like emissaries between the Capulets and the Montagues. Finally, the night of the canine connection fell due. Simon had Toro at the groomer on Second Avenue all afternoon, and he looked it. His coat glistened without a short hair out of place, and the thick, white coat conditioner did its job with alacrity and perfumed efficiency. The great stud was ready for Westminster, if necessary. He stood in near-perfect conformation with all four legs spread apart, all male, all ready. And then he vomited on his anxious owner's black patent boots. He did that sometimes. Nobody ever knew why, but the vet once attributed it to nerves. Simon's trousers, his socks, his leg . . . a mess. He bit his tongue and inner lip several times as he viciously chewed gum and changed clothes. At last, the two swains were at the elevator checking themselves out in the hallway mirror as they waited for 18 to flash to 5 and let them in and cart them away.

They hit the street and walked to First Avenue in an effort to hail a taxi. She was six blocks away and Simon didn't want to give the city an opportunity to spoil a promising evening. Under his arm he had a wooden sampler box of champagne splits resting in a blanket of red satin. It was an evening of new beginnings and certain discoveries, and it just seemed like the right gesture. Many cabs with their empty lights on the roof slowed down as if to pick him up but raced by quickly once having seen the barrel-chested bull of a dog on his thick leather lead. The two studs simply kept walking toward Lisa Lorna's building, having given up the luxury of riding. With the exception of a small dog splat on his black shoe, they arrived safe and near spotless.

The doorman was expecting Brace and Dog and ushered them to the elevator. The doors slid open at the thirtieth floor and they found themselves being let into Lisa's place. She had been standing at her open door waiting to let them in. She seemed as eager as Simon and made the biggest fuss over Toro than he had ever gotten before. The dog just stood in place as if being examined for a hernia with his tongue hanging out and slurping now and again as he breathed heavily from the long walk. Simon handed Lisa the wooden box and instructed her to place it in the fridge. She opened it and cooed, "Let's have a toast . . . to them . . . the lovers!"

"Great."

The room was all peach and satin in a Louis-the-Someone period, and the puffy pillows hissed downward three feet as Simon sat and immediately sank deep into the frame of the couch. Lisa returned with two stemmed glasses shimmering with the golden wine and offered one to the low-riding Simon. She sat on an armchair and for some reason did not sink. He felt as if he was being interviewed for a job. Toro plopped himself at Simon's feet and casually glanced around the room.

Simon winced. "Are you sure Cushion is ready?"

"I'm sure."

"Toro doesn't seem to be responding to the . . . ah . . . aroma of heat. He should be very interested by now, and he doesn't seem to be."

She sipped her champagne and said quickly, "Oh, don't worry about that. I had to spray her with a special atomizer so that the management of the building wouldn't evict me. Believe me, when the time is right, he'll know it." She winked and sipped from her glass again.

The young man drank from his glass, too, but took more in with his eyes than he did with his mouth. He couldn't look away from Lisa, who was especially appealing that night. Under the circumstances, however, she could have been working under the hood of a Mack truck and been appealing to him. The room was hot and his neck was wet with sweat as the gold coin suspended from his large gold chain irritated the few black hairs showing through his exaggerated V-neck shirt. His bright blue pants were tight, and he kept checking for embarrassing, involuntary responses. Lisa was ruffled at the neck in a pale yellow summer dress with tiny white cotton dots that were all that blocked Simon's vision. She took his very breath away. He was sitting at a fixed race, and he held the winning ticket.

"Hey, I've got an idea. Why don't we get those two honeymooners together instead of prolonging their agony."

Lisa giggled and added softly, "I've got a better idea. Let's watch them. Instead of shutting them off in a room by themselves, let's bring them out here in the living room. We'll dim the lights and . . ."

Simon tried to get up from the depths of the couch and failed as he added, ". . . and turn on the music . . ."

". . . and we'll give them romance by candlelight," she finished with a soft, throaty laugh.

Lisa floated out of the room to get Cushion as Simon screwed himself out of the couch and went around turning out the lights. The FM was tuned to a soft music station from New Jersey as a cool breeze blew through the windows. She returned from her bedroom holding her spaniel by a leash in one hand and balancing a lit candelabrum with the other. She set the silver piece on a plate on the white oval dining table and walked Cushion over to the couch, where she joined Simon. With warm, wet hands, Simon stroked the lovely dog and deliberately unclipped her leash from the collar and in a fluid action commenced to unbuckle the collar itself.

"There," he said in a slow, low voice. "It's all off."

Taking her cue from Simon, Lisa began unbuckling the large, thick metal-studded collar of Toro. In a slow motion, both dogs were free. The handsome couple then sat back against the couch, both with their legs tucked beneath them, and relaxed in anticipation. Cushion walked out in the middle of the carpeted floor and scratched herself from behind. Toro remained at Simon's feet, first looking at the dog and then looking at Simon.

"Go ahead, boy. It's okay. She's waiting for you."

Toro slowly moved from his spot and walked toward the waiting Cushion in well-defined movements. In that moment, Lisa clutched Simon's left thigh with both her hands. With hot darts piercing his body he placed his arm around her shoulder tenderly and gave her a flared nostril. She flared back. Toro stood over the lying Cushion like a gloating Hun and licked his lips. He poked his head beneath her tail and whimpered a muffled cry. Cushion swiftly swayed her tail from side to side and waited for another pass. The big Boxer slowly turned, walked back to his master's feet, and slumped down to the floor.

"Hey, what the hell's the matter with you, anyway. Go to it, man. It's there waiting for you. Move. MOVE!"

Lisa removed her hands from Simon and said, "Take it easy. Maybe she just doesn't turn him on or something. Maybe he's sick. Maybe he just doesn't like girls."

The mood changed and Simon blurted out, "What do you mean 'doesn't like girls'? There's nothing wrong with that dog! I wish I had as many women as that dog has had. I'll tell you what's wrong here.

You and that stupid feminine spray. Your atomizer. You're not supposed to spray anything into a dog that's going to mate. They like that smell. They need it."

She tugged her dress to her body with a snap and answered, "If you're going to be vulgar, I'd rather you'd leave. LEAVE NOW!"

Simon rubbed his hand against his forehead and made a desperate attempt to salvage his gurgling biology. "Look, why don't we give them a little more time?" He started to laugh a little as he continued, "We can rub that ridiculous spray deodorant out or wash it out . . ." With each new word he became more involved with stifling his laughter, which was starting to gush out. In an instant he became hysterical, and soon he was laughing uncontrollably. The more he laughed, the angrier Lisa got. She grabbed Toro's leash and collar from the floor and shoved them into Simon's hands. By this time he was in an uncontrollable fit of gagging laughter. She pushed him toward the door. Tears were spilling down his face as he tried hard not to double up. She opened the door and went back for the dog. With a swift boot from behind, she shoved both Toro and his master out into the hallway.

"You're a drag, you know that? And your lousy dog's a complete turn-off. You're both a pair of impotent, celibate, incompetent fumblers. Come back when you've both had a little more experience!" She slammed the door but could still hear the hysterical laughter all the way down the elevator shaft. "Big deal! Who needs it?" she muttered as she snuffed out the candles.

Toro was a normal, healthy dog with no sexual difficulties. The same was true of Cushion. It is a natural part of a dog's life to mate and to reproduce puppies, but every species in nature has been programmed to conform to its own unique set of behavior and circumstances related to sexual activity. So delicate is the process that if any of the conditions necessary are tampered with, the mating will not take place. When inexperienced humans attempt to mate dogs and violate the necessary procedures, not only is there no consummation, but the animals come away frustrated and possibly harmed psychologically.

Clearly, there is much transference of human thought, emotion, and drive involved in sexual liaisons arranged by amateur dog owners. The tendency would seem to be to apply to the dog ideas peculiar only to the needs and appetites of humans. There is little that dogs and humans have in common sexually, and yet the issue is too often forced.

A male dog becomes sexually mature anywhere between six and eighteen months depending on the breed and the individual dog's physiology. The larger the breed, the longer it takes to reach maturity. The American Kennel Club does not register puppies unless both parents were at least one year old when mating. The female is considered mature when she experiences her first estrus cycle, commonly referred to as "heat" or "being in season." Here again the breed and size of the dog affects maturity, which is reached between six and twelve months.

The sexual behavior of wild canids differs greatly from that of their domestic cousins. Wolves and coyotes are essentially monogamous and mate with one female for life. Female wolves experience one estrus cycle a year, while dogs experience two. In an extended pack the leader sometimes will not breed so that he'll have more time to fulfill his responsibilities for pack survival. In such cases, he will leave breeding to lower ranked males.

Because dogs have been domesticated for so many centuries, their sexual behavior varies greatly from the wolf and other wild canids. Feral dogs will breed indiscriminately, but unless a dog has lived in a kennel or pack situation, he has not had the opportunity to learn proper sexual technique through observation. Confinement and close contact with humans have somehow rendered many male house pets hesitant and unassertive in breeding situations. This is not to say that a dog on the loose will not successfully mount a wandering female in heat. Many dogs must be guided and instructed during their first mating. Some domesticated females become frenzied in their first sexual encounter. This is not at all natural to the dog, but is nonetheless common. Timing is also of great importance. If a male is thrust into a situation with a female who is not yet at the receptive moment of estrus, she will behave in a very aggressive manner. This tends to permanently affect the male's attitude toward mating if it is his first experience.

It is customary to bring the female to the male on his home ground. In the wild only the male claims territory. There must be some time allowed for the two animals to become acquainted through the wire of separate kennels, runs, or cages. The male should not be allowed to eat two hours before mating, and both animals must be toileted before being brought together. Noise, audience, afternoon sun, and all forms of distraction must be avoided. Once the animals are introduced to each other they can be left to perform sexually; however, they must be observed to be certain that they have successfully mated. Here the knowledgeable breeder knows that assistance is very often required, and knowing what to do and when to do it is based on knowledge gained from years of experience. Entire books have been written on the subject of breeding dogs. It is not within the purview of this work to adequately explore the subject. It is important to understand the principles of pack behavior when it comes to sex. In a pack, a male is designated as leader because of his size, strength, courage, and ability to lead. He claims territory, finds prey, leads the others in making the kill, selects a mate and propagates. Even the most timid of domestic dogs bases his behavior on these principles. This is especially important when breeding dogs.

When breeding dogs, there is absolutely no value in doing so unless your intention is to produce a dog as good or better than the one which is being bred. The striving for breed perfection is an honorable and worthwhile goal. There can be no other reason that makes sense in a society that can no longer humanely sustain the present pet population. There are already more dogs than there are homes for them. Breeding puppies for fun or profit is less than useless; it is ignorant and inhumane. If puppies are brought into the world for the benefit of a child's education, what is that child learning if the dogs end up in decompression chambers or out on their own scavenging for food in garbage cans?

Allowing dogs to mate when there is no reason for it other than some hidden significance to the humans involved is mindless. It is quite clear that male dogs do not have to be bred in order to live full and happy lives. It is best never to introduce a male house dog to sex (arranged or otherwise) if he is not to function as a constant stud. The typical dog will not miss what he has never had and will in all probability not experience any frustration. For the male that is constantly mounting human legs, vertical objects, or children, the best and most humane solution is castration. A castrated male dog is a wonderful pet that becomes sharply focused on his human family. It has been the experience of many dog owners that their male house dogs have had certain changes of personality after one or two matings. They can become more dominant, more territorial, less playful, less tolerant. This is not always the case but it remains a possibility and should be considered before allowing a house pet to breed.

The sexuality of the female is much different. Unless she is spayed, whether she likes it or not, she will come into season twice a year and experience a hormonal and chemical change in her body at that time. A female usually experiences her estrus cycle every six months, and it normally lasts a total of twenty-one days. During the first week there is a bloody discharge which becomes somewhat colorless in the second week and disappears during the third and final week. This happens whether the dog is ever mated or not. During the

When breeding dogs, there is absolutely no value in doing so unless your intention is to produce a dog as good or better than the one which is being bred. *Carol Benjamin*

three weeks of estrus, twice a year, it is necessary to sequester the animal so that no males can get at her. The best method is to board her at a kennel. If she is to remain at home, she should be kept under lock and key so that there isn't the remotest chance of her darting away and mating with a neighborhood dog. If the dog is not going to be shown in the ring or bred for puppies, having her spayed between six months and four years of age solves all problems pertaining to sex.

Toro and Cushion may or may not have been meant for each other. But the manner in which they were brought together (not to mention the reasons) made it an impossibility. Unfortunately, they were made to suffer far more from the unsuccessful mating than their frivolous owners.

M. Siegal

7

Kids and Canines

WITH a little caution life is not too difficult when a newborn baby enters a home with a resident *best friend*. After proper introductions and a sniff-'n'-see session, simply keep the dog and the infant separated unless someone is in the room monitoring the situation. Even a well-intended dog can injure an infant. If the dog is a decent sort, and most are, he will quickly accept the baby as a new member of the family and become somewhat protective and even responsible for the child's safety. But nothing stays the same, and babies become crawlers, walkers, and runners. Dogs . . . well, dogs just get older.

When a very young child first begins to crawl, the family dog gets a wee bit nervous about it. He doesn't want to hurt the innocent creature, nor does he want his person or his possessions disturbed in any way. An even-tempered animal will do his best to avoid conflict by stepping around the creepy crawler. He might even be amused and accept this new wrinkle as a game in which he can participate. But when the babe dunks a little hand in the dog's water bowl, the dog's only recourse is to shove the child away or look to the adult human for help. With proper supervision, a crawling baby can be encouraged to stay in one or two rooms in which the dog is not allowed, and that will save the day.

Things change slightly once the baby grows into a novice toddler and begins to take those early first steps. The one-year-old wobbles and shakes as it does its own version of the Frankenstein monster. The child begins to sway and reel and then fall flat on its diaper. When a baby first begins to walk, there is little or no physical control over direction or speed. There is only the most fervent desire to propel forward. This then begins to cause trouble for the family canine. If he happens to be in the same room with a baby trying to walk, he cannot be sure where to go that's safe from the little kicks and two-steps. The child comes barreling down the kitchen floor like a little mechanical toy out of control and more than likely will step on the dog's resting snout. Even so, the patient dog, responsible leader that he is, will make every effort to dodge the tiny marcher and find a way to avoid a collision.

Between two and three years, the toddler has mastered the art of walking and is now in great need of moving those legs fast and furiously. There is much energy to be expended. A small living space or a confined child on a rainy day is hellish for a dog just trying to get along.

It was an especially sunny day for February. The glaring winter light was melting the icicles off the apartment-house canopy at a steady rate. The sidewalk was sparsely covered with melting slush, the kind that catches in the cuffs of trousers. Too hot for boots, too wet for leather. A fine day for coming home with a new life. The baby was pink, but the cocoon of a blanket was blue and blue satin. Welcome to the world, Timothy Starn. His dad cried at the moment of his delivery, thus rendering himself useless as a natural-childbirth coach. But Woody did manage to photograph his newborn son anyway. Hilary was forced to do her own counting as she breathed to stay ahead of the painful contractions. It was a normal birth, free of complications, thank God, and both parents were very proud of themselves. They had given up coffee, whisky, cigarettes, aspirin, artificial sweeteners, automobile fumes, and the purple ink stamped on the sides of beef, all to enhance their growing fetus's chances at the moment of retrofire and reentry. Their obstetrician laughed, but the pediatrician thanked them.

The doorman grinned from ear to ear and stole a peek at the blotchy little face sleeping under the bonnet as he let the Starns into the building. The three of them were now an official family unit according to the census takers. The self-service elevator whisked them upstairs quickly to the sixth floor and as a favor did not take its usual circuitous route to the basement laundry-room first. They unlocked the door to their small four-room apartment and damn near slipped on the freshly waxed hardwood floor. Apples had to run for his life because the three of them would have certainly fallen on him. It was a bad sign, but the good-natured dog refused to accept it in that light.

In the parlance of dog lovers, Apples was in the sweetheart category. He was four years old and had lived most of his life with Woodrow and Hilary Starn in their very comfortable apartment. He was born on a farm and was the progeny of a casual mating between a Golden Retriever and a shepherd-collie. The Golden Retriever, his mother, had a very nice life on the farm; she was allowed to live in the house even though her job was keeping the horses company.

It was winter when she whelped, and it was a small litter—only three pups. Her family had set up a stall of her own and matted it with over a bale of hay. The temperature had dropped to zero or less and things got terribly cold in the barn. As a result, the proud mother and her litter were taken into the cavernous farmhouse to keep warm. One little puppy had somehow wandered away from the warmth of his mother and couldn't find his way back in his blind puppy state. He started to yipe incessantly and was found in the winter-apple bin. He had splatted over several of the best-looking ones. From then on he became known to the family as Apples. All of the puppies were coddled and played with and thoroughly enjoyed over the long, cold winter months. It was good for them and good for the folks.

Spring arrived late that year and brought with it the Starns, who were trying to make their fantasy come true about a piece of country property. They couldn't come anywhere near the price of the farm, which had just gone on the market, but they did go home with a puppy. Riding in the back seat of their Volvo was the little tyke who resembled a cross between a coyote and an apricot. He was now Apples Starn.

Life in the city was very much to Apples's liking, even if it was different in many ways from the life of his childhood. He never did get to learn much about those huge four-legged critters that his mother fussed with so much. Now and again he had a vague recollection about large expanses of land where a dog could run to his heart's content. Sometimes when the sweet dog was in a very deep sleep, his legs made jerky motions as if they were running. And indeed he probably was somewhere in the purple mist of another world, running through the freshly cut winter grass, trying to catch up with his beautiful mother who was in another pasture, chasing the horses. Whenever he woke from such a dream, he would stroll to his food and water bowls, sniff them just to be sure they were intact, and curl up again between his own Scots plaid blanket and the warm, soft carpet. That was his world and he liked it just fine. The Starns were a nearly perfect couple and loved him like a son. Everything was set up to his liking until that morning when they returned home from the hospital with the newest member of the family.

It took an hour or two for the commotion to settle down once they came in with the little creature who began to scream and howl the moment they entered the apartment. The crying at first frightened Apples, but once he realized there was nothing to fear, he settled down to accepting it as a mere irritant. He patiently waited for his family to stop fussing about with that awful new animal so that they could praise him for something, for anything. He was in desperate need of a good praising and a head rub. After a while he found his hard rubber ball and carried it to Woody in his teeth, and plopped it in his lap. "Geez, not now, Apples. I've got a headache." The orange-blond dog retrieved the ball with his mouth and looked for Hilary. She was moving so fast between the linen closet, the chests, and the storage closets that the dog couldn't even catch her eye, much less her lap. In desperation he hopped up on their night table and deposited the chewed-up ball into the bassinet where the baby was patiently waiting to have his hunger looked after. After the initial shock, the baby looked wide-eyed at the dog face peering in at him and immediately went to sleep. Hilary screamed when she saw the dog leaning on the edge of the bassinet with his two front paws. Woody came running into the room in a mad dash. Apples leaped high in the air and acrambled to the living room, behind the couch where he commenced to pee a quart and a half. He did not come out for the rest of the day.

In the years that followed, Apples made his peace with the child who started out as Baby Starn, progressed to Timmy, Timothy, and now, almost three years old, Tim. It's not so much that Tim made

Photo by M. Siegal

Apples crazy as that he occasionally upset him. A four-room apartment is not an overwhelming living space. From the very beginning, Woody was forced out of his den so that it could become the nursery. He had to sell his old rolltop desk and buy a Sears mini-size desk for a corner in the living room. It was there he did such things as work out his income tax and other paper work that he took home on occasion. Hilary did her sewing on the kitchen table now, and even Apples vacated his favorite spot next to the heat pipe in what was now Tim's room. Everyone had to compromise and sacrifice for the young master of the house. Apples tried not to mind.

It's not that Tim didn't love the dog. It's that he had his needs and the dog had his own. As a matter of fact, Tim was constantly hugging the beleaguered animal and making grand statements of his feelings. His favorite activity was sucking the tip of the dog's tail and soaking it till it dripped with saliva. Apples was constantly moving his tail away, tucking it under his haunches, and sitting on it. But the good-hearted dog made a game of it and was amused at Tim's attempt to grab it during these sessions. The dog's answer to Tim's learning-to-walk period was to spend the better part of the waking hours under the kitchen table. But even there he was subject to Tim's probes. There was really no place in the small apartment where the dog could get away from the toddler for very long. His only defense was when Woody or Hilary stopped the little boy's affectionate pursuit.

Apples was now seven years old and Tim was about to turn three. What really began to grate on the dog's nerves was Tim's need to run and expend energy. On a really needful day, particularly if he didn't get to go outside, Tim would grab one of his building blocks and throw it across the entire length of the living room into his own room and then rampage across the floor in hot pursuit of the thrown object. This was not very relaxing for the dog. It was the last thing he needed now that he was getting older. At one point he jumped into the air and caught the block with his teeth, ran under the big bed with it, and chewed it to splinters. At first Tim was amused, but his giggling stopped when he saw what had happened to his possession. Then he began to cry. There was a small commotion that ended with Tim going to his room and Apples being locked in the bathroom as punishment. Hilary sat down at the kitchen table over a cup of coffee and a migraine.

Apples was let out of the bathroom that evening when Woody got home. He took the dog out for his walk and stuffed four biscuits in his mouth once they were outdoors. The dog loved them. Woody felt terrible about the incident. He and Hilary loved the dog almost as much as they did Tim. They simply weren't sure where they were all heading.

It rained the next day, and Tim had to play indoors again, much to the misery of Apples. Around eleven in the morning, Tim took the paper hat that his mother made for him and the cardboard sword and decided to play march. With the sword raised high in the air and his hat cocked to one side, he got behind Apples and forced the dog to move ahead of him for fear of being stepped on. After ten minutes, Hilary had to get off the phone and respond to a horrifying shriek coming from Tim. She ran into his room and saw him crying bitterly as Apples cowered in the corner with a guilt-ridden look on his face. His ears were slunk back behind his skull, his tail between his legs as he hugged the wall.

Tim removed his hand from his cheek to show his mother where he had been bitten. It was a neat set of puncture marks caused by the dog's incisors, the row of front teeth. The skin was broken, red and slightly cut. The boy was not bleeding, but blood was showing from the puncture wounds. What scared Hilary the most was the location of the wound. It was approximately one inch below Tim's left eye. She scooped up the boy in her arms, wrapped him in her coat, and dashed to the emergency room of the nearest hospital.

That night Hilary explained to Woody that Tim had been given a tetanus shot, which he thoroughly hated, and that the wound had been cleaned with an antiseptic. Tim had wanted a bandage, but the doctor stuck a small Band-Aid on his wrist to please him. The little boy went to bed early without eating much dinner. Both Hilary and Woody toyed with their food without finishing. They were extremely upset.

"What'll we do about Tim's birthday party?" asked Hilary.

"Well, we're not going to cancel. We'll just have to board Apples until it's over."

The two of them sat quietly for a while, avoiding the obvious. They watched television for a short while to break the heaviness in the air. Woody ran to the phone and began dialing.

"Who are you calling?" she asked.

"The Parson farm. Maybe they'll take Apples back."

Hilary began to cry and shake her head. Woody hung up the phone and went to his wife to comfort her.

"I got an operator. The number's been disconnected. They must have sold the farm. I guess we'll just have to cope with the problem in some way. Don't worry, honey. Apples isn't going to be thrown away."

The following week, Timothy celebrated his third birthday with a splendid party for him and his friends. Everyone was there except Woody and Apples. They went out for a long walk in the park. It was the least they could do for a three-year-old's birthday party.

Apples was not sent away. That was the least they could do for a seven-year-old dog who loved them all very much.

It is a very serious matter when a dog takes to biting a small child. It is usually at the point where parents draw the line and rid themselves of the problem by heartlessly ridding themselves of the dog. In almost all cases of this sort, there is no justice for the dog. He is pushed and badgered, and his position is usurped to an unbelievable degree until he has no choice but to start pushing back in order to survive. Unfortunately, his survival is in greater jeopardy when this happens. A dog that loses his home winds up in a poor second home or none at all. He is cut off from the ones he knows and loves and suffers great emotional trauma and worse. Many dogs who lose their homes find themselves in the pound. From there it's a short walk to the decompression chamber where they are killed.

This situation gets to the very heart of the dog's nature, and understanding it is being able to empathize and try to do the correct thing for all concerned. Dogs, like wolves, are animals that live in a pack or communal structure. The pack can be likened to a nation that works together and strives to make life safe and prosperous for all its citizens. But in order to achieve those goals everyone must play a part and serve some function. As I've said, a social order develops, based on strength, courage and leadership abilities. Once the social order is established, the pack goes about the business of defending territory, finding prey animals and securing food by bringing down the strays and dying members of the prey herds. Mating takes place, cubs or puppies are born, and they are raised, fed, and protected. The pack replenishes itself with new, young population . . . life goes on. This

all happens within the discipline of rigid social strata. Only when the leader can no longer perform is he deposed and replaced with another, usually younger and stronger. A sick or wounded member of the pack is treated like one that loses its rank. It is either torn to pieces or abandoned for the sake of the survival of all. A wolf pack or wild-dog pack is only as large as the territory that can sustain it. Every member must pull his weight and take his earned place in the social structure.

Despite the fact that domestic dogs have never lived with those conditions under such austere terms, and despite the fact that domesticity has brought them very far from that stark life-style, it is part of their inherited behavior. All dogs have such genetically organized traits and inherit these values and behaviorisms, even the gentlest house pet.

The pet dog uses the human family as a substitute for the pack unit. This is true even if the family consists of one dog and one human. In most cases the dog accepts the subordinate position and the human or humans take the dominant position. It is an interesting phenomenon when the dog takes the dominant role and the human or humans take the subordinate role as was the case with Mortimer. It happens very often in the pet/family configuration. Once the dominant/subordinate figures have been established, it is extremely difficult—if not impossible—to change those positions without great upset or even psychological disturbance to the dog.

In the story about the Starn family, a situation is posed that frequently occurs in families. Apples had been a member of the family for four years, long before a child entered the picture. A pack of three was established. Apples was placed in a subordinate role for many reasons, not the least of which had to do with his size, his effectiveness in tending to matters connected to his own survival, and to his seniority. From Apples's perspective, Woody and Hilary had taken possession of their apartment or territory long before he arrived on the scene. He was low man on the totem pole for a variety of reasons, all of which made perfect sense and were absolutely acceptable. It is the primary reason that dogs live in human society with such great success. However, a new member of the family came to live with them. To Apples, this child was no better than a cub or puppy, and was regarded as such.

Wild dogs and wolves take excellent care of their young. They nurse and wean their puppies. For a long period of time they will bring freshly killed meat to the den, where the hungry cubs eagerly wait for their meal. Once the young are old enough, they are taken on hunting expeditions and literally taught how to track, kill, and feed off prey animals. In the domestic dog's case, the human is the surrogate guardian and performs all these parental services. This is called *epimeletic behavior*, which means the giving of care and attention. Male wolves are as involved in epimeletic behavior as are the females and often take over some of the responsibilities of rearing the young. In a pack society, "aunts" and "uncles" also help in feeding and looking after the cubs.

Even though an order of dominance and subordination begins to develop within the litter itself, it is quite clear that a cub's or puppy's position within the larger pack structure is definitely a subordinate one. No adult dog or wolf would tolerate the least bit of insubordination from a pup without some form of reprimand such as a cuff on the snout or carrying the offender off by the scruff of the neck with the teeth, or even a controlled bite in a tender area.

Not until the dominant wolf is older and weaker does the younger member of the pack get his way. Then an old or sick member of the pack loses his position by a physical challenge which often results in his death. Old or widowed wolves whose teeth are no longer sharp enough to fight or hunt often become "lone wolves" and live away from the pack, eating what they can scavenge from the leftovers. For these reasons, a change of status is much feared.

In the case of the Starn household, Apples was not threatened when the baby first came home from the hospital. But as the child began to grow (and grow larger than the dog) and gain more status in the family as indicated by his parents, Apples's imprinted behavior came into play. It was the beginning of a challenge to his dominant position over the child, and that became increasingly more of a threat as the little boy grew bigger. Where he was more or less tolerant of the child's physical abuse as a baby, the dog became less and less tolerant from toddlerhood on. Finally, when Tim tried to push him around the floor by marching behind him, the dog made his stand and in an almost reflexive, ritualistic manner met the challenge to his place in the social order. Hence Tim got bitten on the cheek, and nobody understood why. It would be too easy here to say that the dog simply didn't want to be pushed around anymore. The real point is *who is doing the pushing?* Apples might have tolerated this treatment from the adults of the household.

With these factors taken into consideration, it is a simple matter to make those efforts necessary to assure the dog that his position is secure, at least for a while. Once the child's status begins to change, the dog must be gently and gradually introduced to the idea that the youngster will be a dominant figure. This can be accomplished by having the child slowly take over some of the responsibilities for the dog's needs, such as feeding, walking, and even giving refresher sessions of basic obedience commands. If all this is introduced by the other dominant figures, an even-tempered dog will accept it. It is especially important at that time to maintain the same routine of daily events that affects the dog. He must be fed and walked at the same time as usual. More praise, more affection, and more attention than usual is very helpful. There is no reason for the dog to feel challenged if his family is aware of his true nature, and there is definitely no reason for him to lose his home after so many years of loyalty and devotion.

8

Animal Crackers

Dogs and Neuroses

Some dogs are nuts. They wheeze their psychosomatic hacks and coughs until they get you exactly where they want you. Others howl, bark, or snarl until you toss them the boneless sirloin or the strawberry parfait. There are the pacers and the chasers, the snappers and the crappers, and the barkers, biters, and quakers. There are those who run from thunder, attack strangers, quiver in traffic, nasty up the sheets, develop sexual attachments to human beings, and eat grass only to throw it up all over the azaleas. Dogs so inclined are often labeled neurotic, depending on how entrenched they have become in their unusual behavior.

Because of the complexity of the human brain and accompanying emotional system, fine lines of distinction must be drawn between psychoneurotic, eccentric, and individualistic behavior among this higher order of mammalia. Human neurosis may be characterized as a disorder of the personality in which behavior is defensive and often exaggerated. The neurotic person experiences anxiety because of unconscious efforts to solve unconscious conflicts. This may manifest itself in loss of memory, obsessions, compulsions, hysteria, phobias, imagined (or real) illnesses, and, worst of all, depression. Millions of people throughout

Of course my dog can walk . . .

but thank goodness he doesn't have

M. Siega

114

the world suffer from various forms of psychoneuroses but somehow manage to live with them. Neurosis takes its worst toll when the victim is no longer using these behaviorisms as a defensive measure but has, over the course of time, developed them into an implacable life-style. Clearly, abnormal behavior is far more complicated in human beings than it is in animals. Merely defining abnormal human behavior has become as difficult as treating it therapeutically.

In the most fundamental and general terms, it is possible that humans and animals may share the same set of behavior mechanisms that, when disturbed, create anxiety accompanied by abnormal or neurotic behavior. These fundamental disturbances may be related to territory, social structure, and population density. All creatures vary from individual to individual, let alone among species, order, class, and phylum. However, at some level, they appear to be influenced by the same precipitous circumstances.

Subtlety and imagination make human neurosis enigmatic and elusive. Canine behavior is exquisitely clear in its normal state and equally clear in its abnormal or neurotic composition. Canine neurosis can be so clear that you often step in it. The question is: is the behavior as neurotic as it seems?

———————

The only one who never felt pain between Siegfried's teeth was Whiskers, a black cat with white paws. The German Shepherd often carried the cat in its mouth from one place to another without causing the slightest wince or whimper. As a matter of fact, the affectionate cat loved the ride and thanked her four-legged bus with a tap of her claws on his snout. It didn't hurt the big dog, and he accepted the cuff with gentlemanly tolerance. The cat often played with Siegfried by laying on her back and boxing with his snout as he sniffed her and rolled her about with his nose. He was stoic about her claws and took what came with dignity and gentleness. The black and tan Shepherd accepted responsibility and was comfortable with decision making. Siegfried was the head of the house and ran things with efficient authority. His mistress approved because they lived in a high-crime-rate neighborhood.

It was one of those attractive four-room apartments that

Marilyn Hill paid for with more than one-fourth of her monthly salary. It was really more than she could afford, but it made her feel successful and somewhat glamorous. Her pale blue wall-to-wall carpet and white telephone with gold bands around the receiver impressed her friends. Her twice-weekly maid service impressed her mother. And the automatic washer and dryer impressed her dates (because they could shower and wash their underwear). Inside her leather hassock, which was a hollow storage bin, she had stored every copy of *Cosmo* since 1974. Scotch-taped on the inside of her louvered closet door was a headline from a clipping: "CHUNKY IS BEAUTIFUL—IF YOU KNOW HOW TO WORK IT!"

The tenant Hill had to promise her mother that she would buy a large dog before moving from the parental home in Chester, Pennsylvania, without being disowned. She was a secretary in a large corporation that moved its headquarters to New York City, offering her the position of assistant head purchasing agent if she moved with them. She took the big step, rented her luxury apartment on the East Side, and acquired the largest German Shepherd west of the Rhine. Siegfried was a fancy import and had the papers to prove it. He was too large to compete in the show ring and too easygoing for attack work. He was a steal at $900. The large dog-presence pleased Marilyn's mother even though he was not particularly thrilled with her. He would sulk around the nervous, jerky movements of Mrs. Hill and try not to stare at her. It made her uneasy and kept her visits down to one or two a year. Siegfried was pure gold and his mistress adored him.

Whiskers was two years old and Siegfried was three-and-a-half. In the three years that Marilyn lived in her apartment, she never once had a problem with burglary, molestation, or mugging. Siegfried's presence was well known to the neighborhood by his deep, throaty woof that sent chills down the spines of strangers as they passed the apartment door just a little too close for his pleasure. A single woman, alone, had little to fear with ninety-five pounds of furry guardian sleeping atop her bed every night. The slightest indication of an alien presence in the powder-blue apartment set the dog in motion. When Siegfried stirred, the cat leaped from the pillow to the highest surface in the bedroom, always to the top of the chiffonier. The gentle, sweet, and loving Siegfried was transformed into a medieval beast, barking, and slathering to get at the source of the extraterritorial suspect. Only the froth and the spikes were missing. It always scared the hell out of mistress Hill, but she faithfully rewarded him with a loving pat after ordering him away from the door or window or bathroom drip. It was not difficult for her to fall back into her pillow and drift away quickly with a safe smile that bordered just a little on arrogance.

Siegfried was no pussycat. He guarded his lady lovingly, completely. Marilyn was ostensibly the head of the household, but the great Siegfried was its Praetorian Guard. He was king of the hill.

In the years that Siegfried, Whiskers, and Marilyn lived together, life settled down to a very comfortable family style of existence. The relationships developed fully and completely. Each member of the family behaved in a predictable manner to the others, and there was a desirable acceptance and safety in the knowledge of such intimacy. Marilyn did not like strangers knocking at her door, and Siegfried took care of her discomfort. Siegfried did not like being alone, especially during working hours, and Whiskers was the solution for that problem. Whiskers—well, Whiskers just enjoyed her life with the other two and seemed to make the entire household revolve around her. In their own special way, they, too, were a nuclear family. Oh, brave new world!

Nothing could be more important to any dog, especially a dog of Siegfried's age, than predictable consistency and orderly routine. Marilyn hopped out of bed every working day at 6:45, showered, prepared her breakfast, and spent many puzzling hours in front of her bedroom mirror—the one with all the lights that hurt the dog's eyes if he stared into it for longer than a minute. During the hair and face ritual, the dog sat like a sphinx, panting, with his long tongue hanging out one side of his mouth. Whenever some portion of the procedure failed, Marilyn would yell some four-letter expletive and Siegfried would tuck in his tongue, quickly glance at her, and then look away with wrinkled eyebrows (if it can be said that dogs have eyebrows). Her pain was his pain. Her joy was his joy. There was then the quick shuffle at her closet, and out the door. Whenever she left, his heart always sank just a bit. It was like the room's going dark. Poor Siegfried had great difficulty separating his existence from Marilyn's. It was as if they were the same person. However, before he could sink into a drooping state of nonexistence, Whiskers would make a diving attack on his back from some secret perch and cause the dog to forget his bad feeling.

At 6:00 every evening, the two playmates would hear the key

going into the lock, and their ears would prick and their hearts would beat faster as all tongue and breathing activities were arrested. In some mental body-clock, Siegfried's concept of his life had to do with splitting apart and coming together again every sixteen hours. He even understood holidays, weekends, vacations, and an occasional overnight visitor. What was hard for him were those rare, now-and-again nights when his mistress did not come home until the morning. And lately it was happening with a disturbing frequency.

On those nights, Marilyn came home from work at 6:00 as always. She fed the animals and took Siegfried on his walk far earlier than usual. Then there would be a frenzy in the bathroom, yet another one of those awful sessions in front of the bedroom mirror, and finally the ordeal at the closet. The doorbell would ring, the dog's hackles would rise as he attacked the door with horrifying fury, and Marilyn would have to command him to retreat. With restless obedience he would sit in the background as a strange man entered the apartment and embraced the attractive young woman.

The first time it happened, the dog sprung into action and would have done severe damage if his mistress hadn't interceded in time with a loud, shrieking "No!" With hurt and confusion, Siegfried slowly loped into the bedroom and slumped to the floor behind the bed. The door slammed and he didn't see Marilyn until the next morning, when she made a mad dash to dress for work. That night, life returned to normal. However, once or twice a week, the routine was interrupted with the strange man's presence, which meant that the animals would not see their loving mistress until the next morning—and at that for only fifteen minutes. Life was getting hard. Siegfried was getting heartsore.

It's not as though Marilyn had ignored or forgotten her responsibilities toward the animals. As a matter of fact, one could say they were still receiving the best of care. Life had taken a turn for the vital young woman, and things were changing or, at least were in a state of transition. Marilyn was too busy, too involved, too intoxicated with her newfound relationship to fully appreciate that things were quickly evolving into another way of living. Although she was not one to fantasize about true romance, love and marriage or any other pulp fiction about men and women, things were happening, be it chemistry, genetic counseling, the Freudian imperative, natural selection, or inner tennis. Marilyn Hill had a feller, and she liked it fine. The thing about it was that there was no way to explain to the dog that she was having one hell of a good time and didn't want it to stop. The truth of the matter was that it never occurred to her that the dog and the cat were a factor in all this.

Harold Eber was a better-than-average man and a good match for Marilyn. He was the sole proprietor of a small camera shop in Manhattan and a better-than-average photographer. Without deprecation, he referred to himself as an artistic merchant and was proud of the self-anointed designation. Between picture sessions, lab work, and over-the-counter sales, he made a decent living but was practical enough to be grateful for Marilyn's position and the income derived from it.

And so a wedding took place, after which Harold moved into the pale-blue apartment. On moving-in day, Siegfried silently watched Harold lug carton after carton through the front door. He grunted and moaned as Harold dragged in leather suitcases, quadraphonic equipment, house plants, campaign chairs, a framed diploma, a color TV, and a handball trophy. He was definitely a substantial presence. Whiskers hid behind the bathtub. Siegfried did nothing but watch from a corner of the bedroom. He had already been introduced to the man and given him tacit approval. Actually, it was more like temporary permission to come in. The new member of the family had no idea that he was there on a temporary visa and that Siegfried had a wait-and-see attitude. He also didn't understand that there were several codicils to this new social contract, and his was a limited partnership from the dog's point of view.

Like all wedding days, even one that involved moving, it came to an end and proceeded toward dinner and then bed. Throughout the evening, a warm glow permeated the apartment, and the family of four seemed to enjoy the occasion. Harold and Siegfried played stick for a while and spent a pleasant fifteen minutes together. All seemed well with the world.

Wineglasses were drained, the dessert remained in the refrigerator, unopened, and the newlyweds prepared for bed. Harold wore his silk pajamas. Marilyn was already under the blankets. Before Harold could move out of the bathroom doorway, Siegfried trotted in from the living room and hopped onto the foot of the bed and curled up as usual. The dog had gone to work for the night as he always had. The honeymooners laughed. Marilyn tried to shoo the big galumph off the bed, but he would not move. The dog stretched out and rubbed his head against Marilyn's knees. She blushed and

Harold gulped with something between embarrassment and jealousy. He suggested that they try to ignore the dog for a while.

As Harold came to the edge of the bed, Siegfried uncurled his massive body and sprang to all fours. The dog didn't exactly snarl, but he didn't look any too friendly, either. He angled himself between Marilyn and Harold whenever the anxious groom tried to get into the bed. It soon became clear that Siegfried wasn't about to let him enter the bridal bed. The situation continued unchanged for thirty minutes. The air was tense and anxiety-ridden. It was a standoff.

Marilyn commanded the dog to leave the bed, but the mighty defender paid no heed as long as Harold remained in the room. It was reminiscent of King Kong hanging onto the building with one hand and fighting off the gnat-like airplanes with the other. From a special frame of reference, it was romantic and quite touching. From another perspective, it was terrifying, frustrating, and inevitable, taking into consideration the circumstances of the past three years.

Harold finally moved into the living room to claim the sofa. Marilyn soon followed with sheets, pillows, and blankets. They tried to salvage the evening by telling themselves that they had the makings of a good Broadway comedy in this. They closed the bedroom door, leaving Siegfried alone in the bed to contend with his madness by himself. Harold started to clown around as his bride made up the sofa with the sheets. He grabbed her and fell to the carpet in an embrace just about the same moment that Siegfried began to howl. It was a soulful sound which at first sounded like a distant coyote, but grew louder and more urgent, like a neighborhood werewolf. The amorous couple sighed, released each other, and got up from the floor. The honeymoon was over.

Is a dog neurotic if he obeys every impulse that is true to his nature when confronted with a set of circumstances that parallel a similar situation in the wild? We could say that Siegfried's behavior was neurotic because his defense mechanisms were uncalled for. He was in no apparent danger, even though he acted as if he were. He had been encouraged to defend his mistress from those outside their family circle and to regard his territory as inviolate. Once a dog has been taught these things, once a routine has been established, once a reward system has been set up for the performance of certain duties, it is unreasonable to expect a dog to behave differently just because the circumstances have changed.

All dogs have been genetically organized to behave in certain ways under certain conditions. Again, a male dog with leadership quality will be instinctively drawn to a group resembling a pack. He will develop a territory, establish his status within the pack, defend his territory, defend his status (to the death, in some cases). This is normal behavior for all canids. Why, then, should some dogs behave in what seems to be an irrational manner as did Siegfried?

When we look at a dog barking uncontrollably or behaving in an unnatural manner, it is most certainly an animal under stress. The body of the animal has been prepared for some form of action and will either fight or take flight. The body has precipitated the proper chemical changes so that the order of priorities change. The heart pumps faster, the blood pressure rises sending oxygen to the skeletal muscle instead of the skin, the intestinal system, and the kidneys. If stress continues, the physiology of the animal's body is harmed. When the condition is prolonged excessively or is triggered frequently, the animal will eventually collapse or even die. Violations of the animal's needs will cause stress, which in turn will either exacerbate the situation or add new and even more extreme behavior.

Siegfried behaved exactly as he was genetically organized to behave. His training and encouragement went hand-in-glove with his natural inclinations. For three years Marilyn Hill placed him in charge of defending a well-established territory and socially organized pack (or family). His position and duties were absolutely clear. He barked and attacked all intruders as soon as he discerned a threat. He was rewarded with approval and affection for his behavior. He slept atop the bed at the foot and considered that area his nighttime lair. It is little wonder then that he refused entry of this interloper into the inner sanctum of the Hill family.

Three primary elements were brought into play. Harold Eber represented a new and consequently threatening difference in the population density, a violator of the dog's territory, and, most important, an impending threat to the well-established social order of rank. A dog or wolf that has held leader status will not tolerate a challenge to that position without putting up a great struggle. It is a matter of dominance and subordination. Changes in any animal's environment create apprehension, fear, and anxiety, which eventually lead to physical stress. Many so-called neurotic behaviorisms in dogs are a result of fear-provoking changes in the environment such as noise levels, unusual weather, harassment of all sorts, additional population, territory violations, and changes in pack structure.

It is quite clear that Siegfried's refusal to allow Harold entry to the bed was not based on some human emotion such as jealousy or from some unnatural sexual attraction to Marilyn. The dog was simply doing his job as usual. Nobody explained the change to him or took his possible reaction into account. Similar problems often occur in a parallel human situation, and the adults go into shock when the children refuse to accept a new member of the family. Stepparents and newborn siblings often have a hard road to hoe.

Siegfried should have been introduced to Harold on a subordinate/dominant basis. Over a long period of time, Harold could have behaved in a dominant manner with the dog by placing his leash on his collar and taking him for walks, giving him practice obedience commands, feeding him, grooming him, and all the other activities connected with his needs. If the dog had been obedience trained, Harold could have run him through his paces at every opportunity with gentle authority. A relationship would have developed with the dog eventually regarding Harold as a member of the pack structure who is higher up on the social scale.

When it was first decided that Harold would be moving in, Siegfried should have been ordered off the bed and given a new sleeping, guarding position in the living room. A large basket, box, or blanket could have been made available as a new lair or private territory. Once the dog accepted this change, Harold's entry into the household would have been somewhat easier for all concerned. The changes in Siegfried's life-style should have begun long before Harold moved in and therefore not been associated with his presence. A dog makes no distinction between the demands of a changed domestic situation and his instincts. It is the business of the dog owner to manipulate the environment so that the dog can be himself without having to lose his home. Siegfried's refusal to allow Harold into the bed was irrational but not necessarily neurotic. However, had he been punished for his behavior, he might have become irretrievably neurotic.

Poor Harold was forced to sleep in the living room until a

Tom O'Shea

professional trainer was able to work with both of them. The technique was to run man and dog through an accelerated basic obedience course so that Siegfried became conditioned to accepting Harold as a dominant figure. At the same time, the trainer corrected the dog every time he attempted to get up on the bed. After each correction, the dog was walked to his new sleeping quarters, given praise, and commanded, "Stay." This all took time and patience.

Biting is not always an indication of mental instability in dogs, either. Neither are other forms of aggressive behavior. However, no matter what the cause, there are more than a few good reasons why it's of vital importance for all dog owners to recognize signs of canine aggression and then to do what's necessary to prevent a dog from biting. Obviously no one wants the family pet to harm anyone. The result of a dog attack is almost always costly lawsuits and medical expenses paid by the dog owner to the victim. The dog owner is held responsible and sometimes must surrender the pet to local authorities.

This is not an apology for dogs that bite—but most dogs who have bitten someone are really not understood and tend to be viewed unfairly in terms of canine behavior. Dogs who bite do so primarily to defend their territory, possessions or position of dominance. Some breeds (and many individual dogs) defend their homes with greater vigor than others and consider their human beings as much their personal property as their chow bowls. But, as any mailman can attest, dogs cannot always understand the difference between intruders and innocent strangers. An innocent stranger can be a child chasing a ball.

A dog will bite either out of aggression or fear. In most instances, the aggressive biter is a male. Fear or shy biters are most often females, although male dogs can also be nervous and fear-ridden. Aggressive dogs view their victims as enemies to be defeated. Fear biters do their damage as a way of defending themselves against an anticipated harm or, in some cases, as an uncontrollable response to something that terrifies them. Biters may also be dogs who have been abused by human beings or other animals, abandoned, tormented, taught to be vicious or suffering from a medical problem (pain can be one reason for a dog to begin biting). A dog who has once been beaten will have great fear of the human hand—and so to put out one's hand to pet such a dog could well invite a nip or worse.

A barking dog never bites? Not necessarily so, but a barker's potential danger can be gauged by the ferocity of the barking and accompanying aggressive behavior. Like humans, many dogs have been genetically endowed with more aggressiveness than is good for them.

A dog who growls and snarls at you from deep within his throat; chases people, bicycles or cars; snaps, nips and bullies is a potential biter. Many dogs snarl if *anyone* goes near their food or possessions, including their owners.

All dog owners should observe and try to understand their pets' idiosyncracies and to learn how to spot early symptoms of aggressive and fear behavior—and then act quickly before the dog actually bites.

One of America's leading dog trainers and a former commanding officer of the Army K-9 Corps, Captain Arthur Haggerty of the *Captain Haggerty School for Dogs in New York City,* says obedience training is the only important cure for dog biting.

"A veterinarian will tell you to castrate an overly aggressive male dog with a biting problem," Haggerty says. "However, it will take at least six weeks to realize a change in any dog's behavior after the surgery. I can have the dog trained by then, giving the owner a great deal of control. Castrating an aggressive male dog will certainly help correct his biting problem, but the dog will still need obedience training. Some dogs require both measures. Obedience training is the answer for correcting biting problems in female dogs. When your dog bites someone, you are already six weeks too late."

There are those who believe, misguidedly, that having a dog who bites on the premises is a good security measure, like the presence of an attack or guard dog. But attack and guard dogs, such as those trained for the military, police and industrial security firms, are not simply animals taught to bite. They are professionally skilled, competent, efficient working dogs—and absolutely obedient to their handlers. They do only what they are ordered to do and nothing more. Training your own "guard dog" is like toying with a loaded gun. A dog "trained" by an amateur for protection is not a guard dog at all, but merely a dog brought to a vicious state whose behavior could be unpredictable and disastrous.

A dog who bites is not an asset and must be dealt with as soon as possible in tough, uncompromising terms. *The Koehler Method of Dog Training,* (Howell Book House), is a good book for training a dog with a biting problem, but seeking the services of a professional dog trainer is, of course, the best solution of all.

Finding a job for a dog should be based on what comes *naturally* to the animal.   *M. Siegal*

Abnormal behavior in dogs may lessen or even disappear if the animal is made more active both physically and mentally. Giving your dog a job may be the answer. The average house pet lives a monotonous existence of continual sleep interrupted only by meals, all-too-brief walks, a vacuum cleaner, and possibly a child mounting his back like a bronco. Out of this meaningless existence can come illness, aggressive behavior, shyness, fear biting, insecurity, destructive chewing and, in some cases, a run-down physical countenance. If your dog is bored he is capable of the most obnoxious behavior.

Giving a dog a job is not as difficult as it might sound. It only requires a little thought and imagination. I was once told about a woman who owned one of the Toy breeds. The dog was very yappy, as most Toy breeds are, and liked to act like a guard dog, thinking itself a huge, ferocious beast. It was at its loudest when the woman prepared to leave the house. To combat the noise the woman placed the dog in the "SIT" position. She then placed one of her old handbags on the couch and said to her tiny colossus, "Evelyn, watch my bag!" Believe it or not, the dog sat there for hours every day guarding her mistress's pocketbook. When the woman came home she gave Evelyn a great deal of praise and a nice biscuit. The woman solved the noise problem, but more importantly, she made her dog feel useful and deserving of praise, food and shelter.

Finding a job for a dog should be based on what comes *naturally* to the animal. Obviously, retrievers can carry small objects in their mouths for their owners such as newspapers or small paper bags with lightweight contents, freshly pruned tree branches, or any other light object. (This applies only if the dog is never going to be trained for field trials or actual hunting.) Herding dogs such as Collies, Old English Sheepdogs, etc. can be useful in the rearing of small children. Many dogs, mongrels included, keep small children from wandering off and out of mischief. Some dogs tend to naturally take over the discipline of a youngster and assume responsibility for that child's well-being.

Some of the jobs for dogs are singing along with you, cleaning the floor, pulling the kids on a sled or wagon (using a proper dog harness), learning and performing tricks (see *Dog Tricks,* Howell Book House), or simple house guarding.

Dogs in the service of humankind is traditional, almost to the point of biological truth. They help us hunt, they protect us, they love

127

Dogs must be dealt with as dogs or else one
creates "identity" problems. *Joachim Themal*

us, they guide us when we cannot see, and sometimes function as tools in psychotherapy. Putting your dog to work is not only useful, it is humane and dignified. Take a dog to lunch this week . . . and give him a job.

When you are confronted with abnormal behavior in dogs, look for its cause. It is usually connected with some change in the animal's environment that violates his needs or natural instincts causing fear or anxiety. Correcting the environmental factor is the primary step toward cure. Patience, affection, and gentle behavior modification are the best techniques for effecting change. Sometimes a basic obedience course is the best answer.

Photo by M. Siegal

M. Siegal

9

The Beat Goes On

Aging

Dogs seem to get old suddenly. One day they're playing fetch, and the next day they're limping with arthritis as you notice the gray fur on their snouts for the first time. They become cranky, cantankerous, and downright unpleasant. Older dogs seem harder to get along with, less tolerant, and even snappish. One of the principal aspects of canine aging is anxiety, which causes emotional problems that do have bad effects. But those problems can be alleviated and, indeed, some dog owners have an intuitive understanding of this. They manage to keep their dogs happy and stable for their entire lives.

Most dog owners never realize that old age has caught up with their pets until there is some sign of illness or physical impairment. This is unfortunate because life can be prolonged and the quality of life maintained if the animal is cared for with intelligence and understanding. That requires an understanding of the aging process, how it works, and what to do for the animal as time passes.

Although it is hard to believe, the aging process begins in the average-size dog when he is six or seven years old. This is when full maturity peaks and the metabolism slows down. Cell reproduction begins to falter. The body's skeletal and muscular tissue density begins to slowly reduce in quantity and is gradually replaced by fluids. This means a lessening of the body's capacity to perform its various physical and chemical functions. Your dog may eat more but get less nutritional benefit from his food. Water and fat may accumulate in his body while actual tissue reduces to as little as two-thirds its youthful density. His body may gain weight but actually become smaller. It is, in a word, middle age.

Needless to say, a middle-aged dog, like a middle-aged human, has many, many good years of productivity and happiness available when life is lived sensibly and with a degree of moderation or else the home mortgage business would fail. However, the aging process takes its toll and makes it necessary to place certain limits on physical activities, behavior, and, where possible, abrasive environmental influences. With these slight restrictions, life can be sustained in a reasonable state of health, and your dog can enjoy his full potential of normal longevity.

The older dog cannot be expected to live a full and healthy existence if he is placed in a state of continual anxiety. Anxiety may be a greater killer of older dogs than all sicknesses because it can induce any and all other sicknesses. It is the equivalent to living in a disease-ridden environment. Eventually the animal will succumb to disease and fail to rally the proper immunological defenses to survive. The will to live can exist only when there is a reasonable opportunity to survive. If the cause or causes of anxiety are not removed, then there is no hope for survival, and the will to live disappears.

The causes of anxiety in the older dog are varied, and most are obvious. However, there is an anxiety inducer that few dog owners fully appreciate, and that is the disruption of the normal routine.

———————

Life was about as perfect as it gets for the Stoner dog. He came from a fine line of Siberian Huskies with several champions in his pedigree. His founding stock originated in Russia and was one of the aspects of his pedigree that made his breeder brag the most. At first Charles Stoner hesitated to bring home to his family of six a dog with a better lineage than his own. How could he introduce a dog, albeit a cute puppy, as grand as Count Nicolai de Brugge to his very small children. The breeder wanted his friend Stoner to have this pup because he had a slight fault in his hind legs which would make him wrong for the show ring. The dog was an altogether perfect specimen with that one exception, and the breeder didn't have the heart to destroy him. Stoner decided he could take the puppy if it was okay to call him Nick. The breeder agreed and it was arranged. Stoner also agreed to void the dog's AKC papers to discourage any possible mating. It was the breeder's request that the dog not sire any puppies because of his fault.

And so, Nick started out with a rain check and went to the city to live with Charles and Marion Stoner and their four kids: Lisa, Robert, Fred, and Chuck. Things couldn't have turned out better. The children were all hands, arms, and cheeks as they almost loved their new pet to death. Nick was in heaven. He was four months old when they got him, so he grew up with his four young pals.

Nick turned into a large sixty-pound dog with a rugged, solid body. For a while he seemed taller than Chuck, the youngest of the children. Actually, he never was taller. The children became his special passion along with the nine-room house and the front and back lawns. Over the years he became their playmate, their friend, their entertainer.

Nick was a serious family member with the right instincts for blending in as one of the kids. His size, color and black face-mask scared off strangers whom he treated with a steady stare that was more quizzical than threatening. Once someone was introduced to the bright, energetic companion, he was forever remembered and greeted happily. It pleased Marion, as the lady of the house, to have such a dog who never realized he protected her. They were closer to each other than the others.

His relationship with the children varied. Although Nick had a definite air of superiority, he did not push the dominance business. The animal perceptively knew enough never to confront the issue with all of the youngsters, especially those who were already in their early teens when he was a puppy. Lisa, the eldest of the four, took him over from the very beginning. At thirteen, the girl mothered the little dog. His little, vulnerable body needed help going up stairs and adjusting to street traffic. His need for affection and assurance triggered an instinct in her that had disappeared with her last great doll. If Nick had the key to anyone's heart, it was Lisa's. But as he grew into a juvenile and then adult dog, she changed her manner with him accordingly. She took no funny business and took him in tow. She was the only one in the family who could give him that self-doubt feeling that made his ears lie flat on top of his head. "Did you do this? Okay, Nick, no chicken for you tonight." But when the tone of her voice changed to "You are the dearest person and I love you," his eyes glistened and his tongue panted with slurping joy.

Robert was twelve when Nick was a puppy. The youngster was a big reader, and his approach to pet ownership was to acquire a book about obedience training and take charge with a book in one hand and a leash in the other. It took him seven or eight months to finally accomplish what the course promised in six weeks. By the third month, the playful dog began to take the boy seriously when he was yanked off his feet by the leash during a contest of wills. That was the first and last time he ever confronted Robert. Robert took on the air of a dominant member of the family, and it made the dog feel secure. As long as someone took on that responsibility the dog was satisfied. One always had the feeling that Nick could have demoted Robert anytime he wished. There was a dignified, loving relationship between the two, and it lasted throughout their lives.

Dignity flew out the window when it came to young Fred and younger Chuck. The two boys, ten and six years old when Nick was a puppy, were very involved with practical tricks, toilet humor, and using the dog as an occasional chemistry experiment, an extra in their games, a confederate in their kid crimes. Fred was always leading Chuck astray and drawing him into his pranks and secret activities. Little Chuck adored his older brother and followed him everywhere. This worried Nick. He spent what seemed a lifetime finding the two of them and spoiling their best schemes—such as the time Fred wanted to start the family car and drive it a few feet. He might have hurt himself, Chuck, the car and perhaps someone out on the street.

The two boys entered the car like commandos. The keys had been left in the ignition. Nick became instantly primed when he saw them moving in a crouched position. He slowly rose as he watched them intensely. They opened the car door and slipped inside. This violated the dog's sense of routine. He knew that the boys never went into the car by themselves. As they turned the key and attempted to get the car started without being noticed, the dog dove off the porch in a breathless leap and began attacking the door on the driver's side. His barking was loud and urgent, almost vicious. The light on the porch flicked on, and Charles and Marion came running out to see what was the matter. Fred and Chuck were yanked out of the car and sent to bed immediately. They lost their swimming privileges for the month of July. Nick got to sleep on Marion's side of the bed where her hand occasionally touched his head as she slept. That was the finest reward the dog had ever been given.

In the cold months, during the day when everyone was either at school or at work, Nick's job was Marion. He followed her from room to room as she kept the house clean and straight. When she did the laundry, he would sit by the vibrating washing machine and look at her as if he understood everything she said to him. If Nick could have written a book, he could have told of every emotion and secret thought, wish, and complaint that the lady of the house had. He heard it all. He listened better than a hairdresser and kept his mouth shut, too. She loved him. Marion could not imagine a world without her true and loyal friend and confidant.

For Charles, Nick was the thread that kept the family talking to each other when they were upset or not seeing each other very much. Lisa was dating several boys when she was not doing homework. Robert was busy winning a science award in Middle School, and even the younger boys were deep into their school life. Marion was involved in the activities of her various community groups doing volunteer work and organizing action groups for a traffic light here and a crossing guard there. There was never enough time for Charles to see the pro football game, clean out the garage, or cut the grass at the same time. He settled for a frequent walk with the dog. The two of them explored every square inch of their neighborhood for hours every weekend. Theirs was also a special relationship.

Over the years, Charles kept his word to Nick's breeder and never had the dog mated. They had seriously considered having him altered but decided against it. As Chuck (known by his friends as Charles) said, "for religious reasons."

Lisa went to college, graduated, began a career as a teacher, and then married. At age twenty-seven she became pregnant. Robert was an industrial engineer and lived in his own apartment at the other end of the city. At twenty-four, Fred was a sergeant in the Air Force and stationed somewhere in Texas. He called home often—collect. Young Charles was still at home in his room taking on the demands of Psychology One in his junior year at the university. The class was up to *symptoms of abnormal psychology* and Charles was convinced he had everything from schizophrenia to erotomania. Charles and

Marion became mom and dad and they were doing fine with the exception of an occasional backache and some sciatica. Nick was fourteen years old.

The great old dog moved much more slowly than he did before. He was still a vigorous protector, but the deliverymen obeyed his instructions more out of respect for a senior dog than any other reason. He had a slight limp in his right hind leg from a brush with a moving car, and there was much gray in his dulled coat. The veterinarian cut the dog's rations to almost half of what they once were, and his running days were over. But Nick still followed Marion around from one room to another as she tended to the routine of her much-loved home. Charles still took the old guy out for their weekend strolls around the neighborhood, but never for more than two or three or sometimes four blocks. By the time they got home, the old dog was obviously fatigued.

Lisa and her husband moved back into the family home while they had their baby. It was a joyous event for everybody, including Lisa and her old dog Nick. Over desert one evening, Charles became a little expansive and said he wanted to give his future grandchild something fine, something valuable. A dog, he declared. By God, the child shall have a dog and all of the pleasures and rewards that go along with it. He looked over to the far corner of the dining room and looked at Nick, sitting and quietly participating in silence. Charles experienced a dreadful thought and felt a deep hole in his stomach. "Yes," he said, "we'll get a puppy for the new baby."

A baby boy was brought home from the hospital six weeks later. He was named James. The next day Charles went to see his friend who bred Siberian Huskies and came home with a six-month-old female who had already been dubbed Adelaide. Everyone enjoyed calling her Addy. She was an instant hit. Nick turned away with indifference.

Between the excitement of baby James and Attagirl Addy, Nick was somewhat taken for granted, except by Marion who still allowed him on her side of the bed. For three weekends in a row, Charles forgot about his constitutional with Nick. He was doing what every proud grandfather did; he took his grandson around the neighborhood in his carriage, offering cigars and showing photographs to all the neighbors. Nick stationed himself out on the porch but refused to chase after the preoccupied man.

Addy was a very friendly dog and did her best to strike up some rapport with the crusty old Husky. She made the mistake of approaching him while he was at his food bowl one morning. He let out a deep hissing growl that hadn't been heard from him since he chased a strange dog off their lawn ten years ago. The younger dog froze and got bitten on her upper lip. She bled slightly. The family was upset, and even Marion hollered at him. Nick just slunk off to a corner of the basement and stayed out of sight for the rest of that day.

A month passed by, and Nick became surly and something of a recluse. His gaze seemed focused inward. He no longer solicited loving pats and affectionate glances. He even stopped following Marion around on her housecleaning rounds and failed to show up for washday. She became hurt, upset, and worried when the dog refused to sleep in their bedroom anymore. When they let him, he slept out on the porch. Charles was becoming disturbed by Nick's behavior and was determined to work it out. He decided to leave Nick and Addy alone in the house for several hours one afternoon and allow them to work out their differences, including who was top dog and anything else that was bothering them. It was risky but worth a try. That Sunday everyone cleared out and left Addy staring at them as they left. Nick arose from the floor as soon as he heard the car door slam and walked out of the room. Addy watched him leave and followed him. The time dragged. Charles rushed home one hour earlier than he had set. He couldn't take the pressure. He was worried about Adelaide's safety. When they returned home they were amused to find that Addy was curled up asleep in one corner of the living room and Nick was curled up asleep in the corner of the kitchen. "Nothing happened," said Marion in a dejected one. "Well," said Charles, "we'll just have to live with this situation as best we can. We owe Nick too much to take it out on him now."

Two days later, Marion woke up in the morning and found Nick on the floor next to her bed. He did not move. She knew instantly. The family was gently informed that Nick had left them. He was buried in a state park somewhere in the woods that he and Charles had explored on one of their Sunday walks.

It took three or four weeks before the heaviness lifted around the Stoner house, and once again young master James took the spotlight when he could from Addy. The young dog got all stirred up during a session of exuberant play with young Charles, who had taken time off from his studies. For him it was like old times romping around with another sled dog. In an unexpectant fit of brief hysteria, Adelaide snapped and caught Charles on the thumb. He yelled out in pain and moved away. There was a bit of blood. Lisa chastised the dog and made her leave the room. She went to the kitchen, walked up to her food bowl, and devoured the contents in one quick gorging. In a few seconds, she began to regurgitate.

The next day Charles took her to the veterinarian for a checkup. She didn't look too good, and her behavior was different. Nobody could understand it.

The examination took exactly four minutes when the vet asked, "How old is this girl?"

Charles shrugged and answered, "Eight months, I think. Why?"

The vet smiled and said, "Well, she's a bit young, but it'll be okay."

"What will?" asked Charles.

The vet's answer was a shock. "Pregnant," exclaimed Charles. "Pregnant?!!" He thought about it for a minute and then smiled, too.

Together he and the doctor said, "Nick."

Charles's chest began to push out, and something between a cry and a laugh escaped. "I'll be goddamned. Good for you, Nick."

He went home with the dog, told everyone the astonishing news, and went out for a long walk. He didn't get home till after dark.

As old age catches up with our pet dogs, there is little or nothing we can do to prevent them from getting extra-sensitive to those things that never upset them in the past. This hypersensitivity is part of their nature. Wild dogs and wolves are acutely aware of their failing bodies. With the loss of physical prowess, diminishing eyesight or hearing comes the loss of pack status. A wolf whose teeth are no longer sharp enough to deliver the death blow to a prey animal may not be allowed to enter the hunt, and that means being consigned to eat what little has been left by the others.

A wolf that is not part of the hunt is eventually disenfranchised and left on his own as a "lone wolf." This is a death sentence. Wolves that are wounded, sick, or dying represent a threat to pack integrity. They hinder all aspects of pack existence including defense, hunting, and migration along with the prey animals. Wolves so afflicted are in great danger; at any time the pack may tear them to pieces as survival technique. As a leader of the pack becomes too old or infirm, he is apt to be challenged by a younger member for that position. This is behavior that has been genetically programmed into the animal. It exists in various degrees deep within the genes of all dogs.

It is little wonder then that our pet dogs become moody, grouchy, and hypersensitive as they get older. Dogs do not fear death (as indeed humans should not) because there is no frame of reference for so abstract a concept. However, there is an innate fear that along with old age comes a direct challenge from the social structure to his rights of territory, status, and life itself. Although an older dog's grumpiness may come from pain or discomfort, more likely it stems from some change in his routine that his owner did not recognize as a change.

Nick was getting older. His family did the only thing that creates the greatest anxiety in old dogs. He was forced to live with and adjust to his replacement in the pack structure. Although it was not intentional, it was an extremely harsh change in the old dog's life even though the other dog was a young female and not a true challenge to his status. Nick would have had enough to deal with having a grandchild enter the house, but another dog was more than his nerves could take. It was an attack on his entire nervous system and created a high degree of anxiety. As stated before, anxiety creates physical stress, and if prolonged, will cause collapse and even death. What was most notable about Nick was the valiant effort to regain his position as the young, vigorous leader by asserting his sexual capacity with Adelaide. Sadly enough, it may have cost him his last bit of energy.

A dog pack can be likened to the human family or, in its broadest sense, a national entity. If you are a member of the family or a nonrelated friend of the family, or a citizen of a country, you have various rights and privileges relative to your position in that structure. As long as you do not overstep your position or take that to which you are not entitled, you may live your life in relative peace and harmony. But, if you enter the territory of another pack, or attempt to join a strange pack without an invitation, or enter a country illegally, you become vulnerable to attack either by the pack leaders or by the law-enforcement officials of the offended nation. In large cities, teen-age gang warfare is caused by just such a social reality.

When a pack or a herd of animals becomes too populated for a territory to sustain, natural controls go into effect. Food obviously diminishes, so that hunger and sickness begin to thin out the density of population. Certain behavioral traits come into play that also achieve the desired goal. Some members of a pack or herd will break away, form a new group structure, and then emigrate in search of establishing another territory. Competition for the food and even the territory itself may take place within the social structure. This competition is in the form of a physical confrontation, with the winners remaining and the losers being sent off to wander and possibly die. The losers of such competitions are mostly juveniles, subordinates, the sick, and the old.

The next time you look down into the face of your aging dog, try to understand that some part of his or her brain has a coded message to be on guard and watch for changing signs in the environment. The answer to all your aging dog's emotional problems lies within the definition of the word *reassurance*. Do not change your older dog's routine at all, if possible. Give him or her as much attention and affection as in the past. If possible, give even more of yourself than before. Never leave the dog with strangers. Do not introduce another animal into the household as long as your pet is still living with you. Avoid overnight stays unless you take your dog with you. Try to avoid leaving the dog overnight at an animal hospital unless it is absolutely necessary. Dietary changes should be accomplished very gradually. Increase the number of times you groom your dog. This is a loving activity that not only serves as an opportunity to examine the animal for physical changes but allows you to physically express your feelings.

Reassurance soothes the aging dog and abates those primeval fears which cause so much irrational and unnecessary emotion. Talk to your dog in a gentle, loving tone of voice. Walk with him at a pace that makes sense for his body, not yours. Carry him upstairs, if necessary. Brush him gently every day. Do not subject an old dog to the rigors of very young children. Avoid loud noises. Be firm but not harsh. Communicate with him in some manner whenever something different is about to happen. Of course your dog cannot understand what you say in terms of words. But you'd be surprised how much is understood by the loving tone of your voice.

Meditation is a viable option for those who are interested in the therapeutic effects of this Eastern technique of relaxation and spiritual attainment. Members of all religions are now experimenting with meditation, and many physicians are also recommending it.

Meditation for pets (PM) is easily practiced and offers an opportunity for reassurance—perhaps the best opportunity—that he is wanted, that life is good and that you still love him.

Remove yourself and the dog to a part of the apartment or house where you will not be disturbed for thirty minutes. Advise other members of the household that you do not want any noise or interference. Ask them to take your calls or answer the door. If you and the dog are alone, take the receiver off the hook.

Once the room is quiet, get on the floor so you're on the dog's level. If the animal is nervous or fidgety use a leash and collar. Seat yourself against a wall or piece of furniture and induce your dog to lie down next to you. Small dogs can even be placed in your lap. Flatten both of your hands and lay them over your dog's heart, which is found in the front of the torso, slightly behind the legs. Try to get a sense of his breathing pattern and allow your hands to rise and drop with his expanding and contracting chest movements. This should be very pleasant for the animal. Few if any will resist.

Once your dog is calm, establish a visual rapport. Eye-to-eye contact is fine, but not as a direct stare. For some dogs, this is regarded as a challenge or an invitation to play. Maintain as much silence as possible except when the dog needs to be told that everything is fine. Align your breathing rate to the dog's and breathe together. Pet him slowly as you breathe in unison, keeping one hand over the dog's heart. You may look away or close your eyes and say soothing, loving things to him. You may even whisper his name.

Whatever you choose to do, be certain that it does not distract your dog and get him on his feet. If he gets up, reposition him and start over. Make him and yourself as comfortable as possible. For those who are experienced with meditation, do not be upset if you do not achieve the desired state of relaxation you are used to. This is for the inner state of the dog, not the human. You will know if you are succeeding.

Keep track of the time and break off the first session at fifteen minutes. Gradually extend the sessions until the dog is meditating for thirty minutes a day. Morning sessions are probably best if the dog must endure an entire day of nerve-wracking activities such as children and other distractions. Afternoons are also excellent for meditation. The time is not nearly so important as the level of relaxation and emotional well-being that is achieved. Communication of your love and assurance of his safety can be accomplished through this wonderful lifesaving activity.

The emotional problems of dogs are best understood through the spectrum of animal behavior as it is determined by nature and circumvented by domestication. We have taken dogs and cats out of their natural habitat where their behavior makes sense, increased their population beyond the natural inclination, and demanded of them an adaptation to complex human society. In the humanization of Fido we have given our pets all of the emotionalism that goes along with the comforts and distortions of modern times. As we attempt to soothe our own inner turmoil, so must we help our four-legged alter egos, our mammalian cousins who have been pressed into service. The answer for them does not lie in primal scream therapy or Zen jogging. Pet owners must behave as responsible adults and help their friends with a truer understanding of animal behavior and their own role in creating the emotional problems of their pets. Thus equipped, we may look forward to a new kind of happiness where dogs and people are given the freedom to be themselves.

M. Siegal

Suggested Reading

Campbell, William E. *Behavior Problems in Dogs*. Santa Barbara, California: American Veterinary Publications, 1975.

Carlson, Delbert G., D.V.M. and Giffin, James M., M.D. *Dog Owner's Home Veterinary Handbook*. New York: Howell Book House, 1980.

Dangerfield, Stanley and Howell, Elsworth. *The International Encyclopedia of Dogs*. New York: Howell Book House, 1971.

Fiennes, Richard. *The Order of Wolves*. New York: Bobbs-Merrill, 1976.

Fox, Michael W. *Behavior of Wolves, Dogs and Related Canids*. New York: Harper & Row, 1971.

Howe, John. *Choosing the Right Dog*. New York: Harper & Row, 1976.

Judy, Will. *Puppies and Their Care*. Westchester, Ill.: Judy-Berner Publishing Co., 1972.

——————. *Handling the Mating*. Westchester, Ill.: Judy-Berner Publishing Co., 1972.

van Lawick-Goodall, Hugo and van Lawick-Goodall, Jane. *Innocent Killers*. Boston: Houghton Mifflin Company, 1971.

Mery, Fernand. *The Life, History and Magic of the Dog*. New York: Grosset & Dunlap, 1970.

Morris, Mark L., Jr. *Canine Dietetics*. Topeka, Kansas: Mark Morris Associates, 1975.

Pearsall, Margaret E. *The Pearsall Guide to Successful Dog Training*. New York: Howell Book House, 1973.

Pfaffenberger, Clarence. *The New Knowledge of Dog Behavior*. New York: Howell Book House, 1963.

Ryden, Hope. *God's Dog*. New York: Coward, McCann & Geoghegan, Inc., 1975.

Schaller, George B. *Golden Shadows, Flying Hooves*. New York: Dell Publishing Company, 1973.

Scott, John Paul. *Aggression*. Chicago: University of Chicago Press, 1958, 1975.

Scott, John Paul and Fuller, John L. *Dog Behavior: The Genetic Basis*. Chicago: University of Chicago Press, 1965.

Siegal, Mordecai. *The Good Dog Book*. New York: Macmillan Publishing Company, 1976/Signet Books (paper).

Siegal, Mordecai and Margolis, Mathew. *Good Dog, Bad Dog*. New York: Holt, Rinehart & Winston, 1973/Signet Books (paper).

——————. *Underdog*. New York: Stein and Day, 1974.

Vine, Louis L. *Breeding, Whelping, and Natal Care of Dogs*. New York: Arco Publishing Company, 1977.

Winge, Ojvind. *Inheritance in Dogs*. Ithaca, New York: Cornell University Press, 1950.